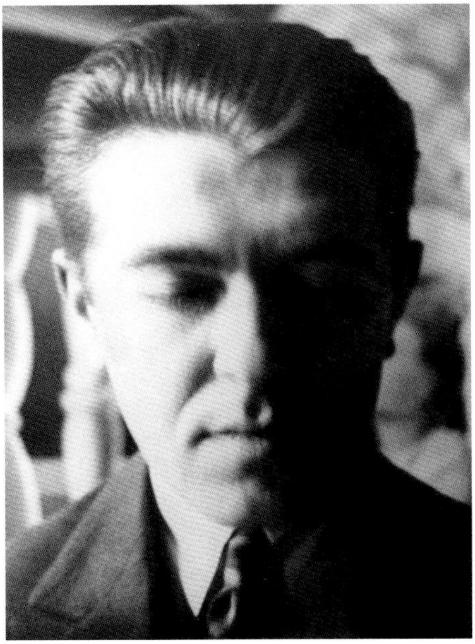

THE MAGRITTE MUSEUM

Julie Waseige

LUDION

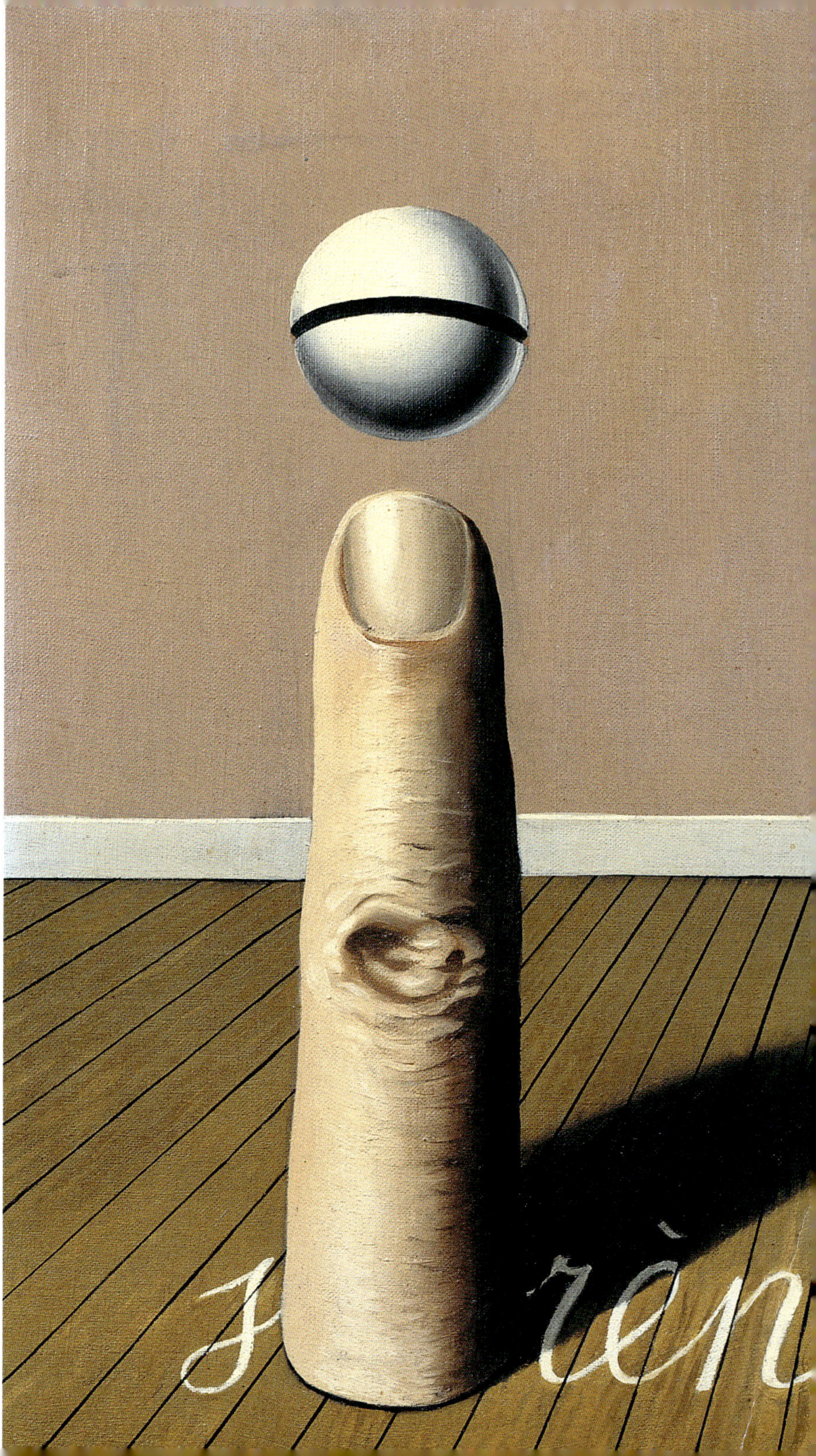

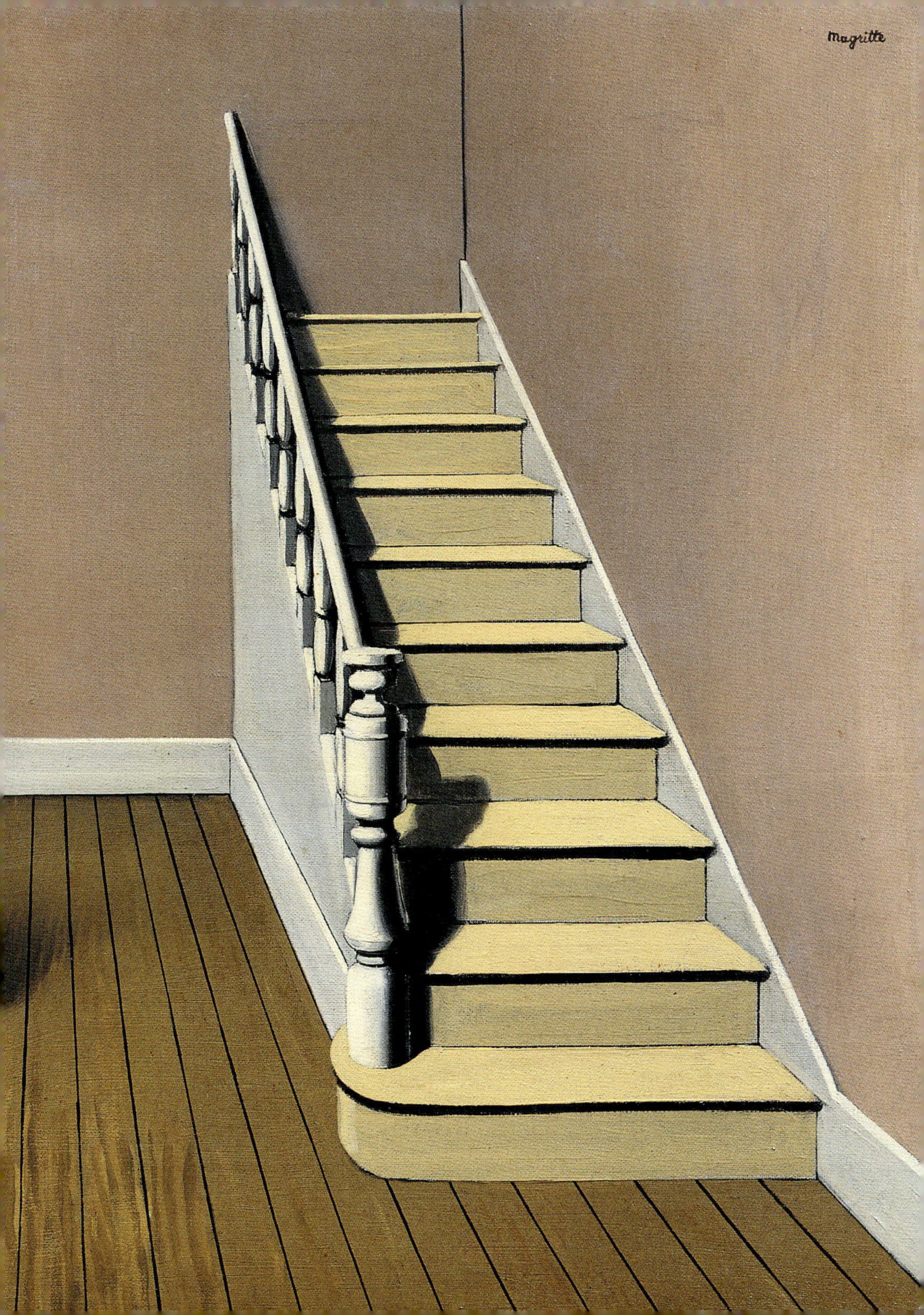
Magritte

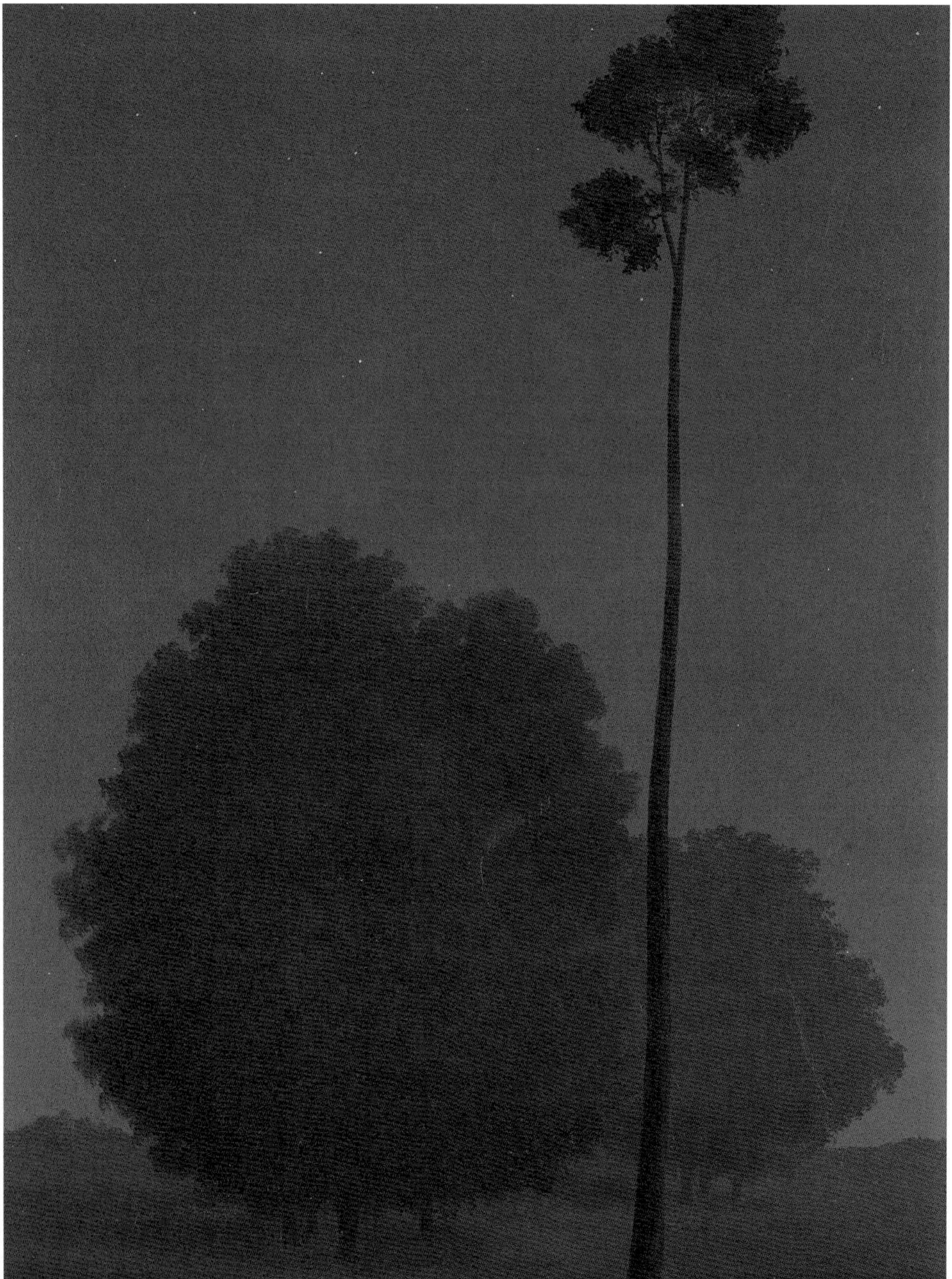

Great Expectations
Oil on canvas, 65.2 x 50.7 cm, 1940

The Magritte Museum
At the Crossroads of Art History

The Magritte Museum is the result of the first instance of skill-sharing patronage carried out in Belgium by the SUEZ group – which has since become GDF Suez – with the support of the Magritte Foundation. It was established through a reinstallation of the collections of the Royal Museums of Fine Arts of Belgium, whose Magritte holdings – consisting of works on paper, paintings, objects, sculptures, archives and a library – are the foremost in the world dedicated to this key 20th-century artist. Foremost not only for the number of works it contains but also for the range of domains included, attesting to the prodigious creativity of an artist who was not only a painter but also a photographer, a poster designer, an amateur film-maker and a true writer. Even so, the creation of a Magritte museum is no cause to hermetically seal his œuvre around a collection that, though abundant, represents less than ten per cent of the artist's production. From the outset, the museum was geared to two parameters: making the museum visit an invitation to reconstitute the thinking of a singular personality who, in a way, extended poetry by means of the image and thereby established the act of painting as a philosophical act; and, through temporary exhibitions, transforming the museum into a place to receive works that, because they are not part of the permanent collection, foster a perpetual redefinition of what is on display and consequently of the installation's underlying discourse.

Through a fluid arrangement on three levels, the Magritte Museum wished to place itself at a crossroads between permanent collection (as presented in the main section of this book), providing a foothold for discovering the work, and temporary exhibition. And it proposed to do this by linking Magritte's work, life and thought in a single perspective, but divided into distinct territories. Despite its obviously monographic nature, this approach nonetheless makes one hesitate, since Magritte was so staunchly opposed to the reduction of his thinking to the determinisms inherent in biography. Beyond this opposition – the philosophical resonances of which largely shatter the artist's posture – what Magritte manifested was more broadly a hostility towards the notion of explanation. This defiant stance was to take its place in the museum in a form patterned after the fascinating model created between 1924 and 1929 by Aby Warburg in his *Mnemosyne Atlas*, a mental space in which, as the image unfurls, it assumes – on its own, in its framing, articulations, connections, juxtapositions and gaps – a discourse based on the obvious. This obviousness is not mere spontaneity (as the catalogue entries that follow show), but an investigation that attests to the density of a way of thinking that arose from setting up a tension between the verbal and the visible, between language and image. This was the guiding principle in an exhibition layout that consequently justified recourse to an atlas, but without neglecting the pedagogical imperative that *necessarily* passes by way of discourse. In this respect, the Magritte Museum coincides with Malraux's pet project of a 'Museum without Walls'. Although universality, as built upon a text's literary authority, may have no currency here, we espoused the modernist tenet of breaking down barriers between disciplines to instil an array of 'escape points' (as opposed to vanishing points) for thought, which requires us to perpetually rethink the subject as a function of the entry point adopted. Following Warburg's lead, this conception retains from Malraux (and, independently of him, a long tradition of art history and cultural history to which Jacob Burckhardt, Aloïs Riegl, Heinrich Wölfflin, Ernst Cassirer, Walter Benjamin, Erwin Panofsky and Georges Didi-Huberman have contributed) the requirement of combining the mechanism of *exhibition* with the need for *demonstration* that passes by way of the book, or more precisely album, where a dialogue takes place between the visible and the readable. One of the Magritte Museum's original features has been to locate this dialogue both inside the museum and on its periphery. Inside, by incorporating only writings of Magritte, which serve as a tool for questioning within a modernist culture from which he took his distance early on (perhaps even to the point of becoming one of the first *post-modern* thinkers); on the periphery, by linking the physical trajectory of the visit to the mental trajectory of the explanation ceaselessly reinvented in response to the works brought together in this space of thought.

The Hôtel Altenloh was built in 1779 to house the Austrian Imperial Lottery; about 1827, it was converted into the Hôtel de l'Europe (where Balzac stayed), and then a jeweller's shop in 1920, before being annexed to the Royal Museums in 1969. In renovating it, GDF Suez's subsidiaries had to deal with the problem of the windows opening onto Place Royale. While this magnificent monumental square merits being visible from the galleries, the natural light these openings diffuse would preclude the presentation of certain kinds of works and documents. It was therefore imperative to restrict the light to less than 50 lux in order not to be held hostage by the curatorial standards proper to the conservation of fragile works on paper.

This was the cost of making the Magritte Museum an atlas, or album, preserving the memory of Magritte's creativity. And this constraint rapidly turned to an advantage. Starting from the idea of an interior vision on which to base the reconstruction of a phantasmagoric world, the museum was designed as a 'black box' inside which the paintings would suddenly appear on the interior walls. In it, the relationship to the work remains exclusive; the work is never treated as a document but exists in its own right and for itself, as a function of the wall opposite the viewer. On the two upper floors, a chronological narrative develops from one painting to the next. The works unfurl in a continuity that, like an album, plays on the dialogical tensions of a double spread according to whether the walls form an angle or face each other. The narrative takes on a cinematic value that capitalizes on the Surrealist principle of surprise. Between full-fledged Surrealism and the 'Vache' period, this applies to the theme of the nude, which, from *Black Magic* to *The Pebble*, presents its evidence without relying on explanations and does so via a layout that at times surprises visitors, at times isolates them in an exclusive relationship with the poetic image.

Endeavouring not to close off our understanding of the painter's approach by restricting it to a single, unvarying selection, the Magritte Museum has opened its walls to works from outside the collection. This led to cooperation with other museums, like the Koninklijk Museum voor Schone Kunsten in Antwerp (which lent *The Sixteenth of September*, among other works), the Museum of Modern Art in New

York (for *The Menaced Assassin*, which rejoined its 'pendant', *The Secret Player*), and the San Francisco Museum of Modern Art (for *Personal Values*), not to mention such signal canvases as *The Field-glass*, *The Listening Room* and *The Memoirs of a Saint* from the Menil Collection, our structural partner. The collection's openness met with enthusiasm among private collectors, many of whom have entrusted works to the Magritte Museum in order to initiate new dialogues or reveal little-known facets of the painter. This constant exchange renews the discourse and makes it possible to perpetually transform what the museum communicates. Neither congealed nor permanent, it invites a reconsideration of the trajectory of the work as a function of the singular links woven between the paintings, drawings and photographs by way of their arrangement in space.

The visual layout that develops gives pre-eminence to the works. In taking their place on the museum's walls, they affect our understanding of the painter, multiplying the avenues of research to be explored by exploiting documents that provide a context. This context occupies a clearly defined place, in display cases arranged so as not to interfere with viewing the works and on screens on the exterior walls that form a sort of second skin for the building. Magritte is subdivided; he ceases to be only a painter and reveals himself as a man and as an agent of Belgian Surrealism. Personal photos re-create an existence without lapsing into the logical impasse of an exhaustive reconstruction. Intimate snapshots are treated as fragments of memory that preserve recollections of bygone days, with their typical seaside vacations and (oft-times eclipsed) friendships. The incorporation of video made it possible to give these encounters a particular setting. Lecomte, Nougé, Mesens, Breton, Mariën and Torczyner bear witness as accomplices who forged the painter's thought and, hence, his work. A series of short video clips enables visitors to reconstruct a network of relationships about which the Museum's internet site provides fuller documentation. The work does not issue from the hand of a solitary genius but takes part in a debate that draws upon the society of its time for the terms of its development. From commercial advertising to anti-Fascist political activism, Magritte's work and thought question the art institution as well as orthodox Stalinism. Further along, the focus shifts to the artist's inclusion in a *milieu*, exemplified through his relationship with the Brussels bourgeoisie gravitating around the Palais des Beaux-Arts, whose portraits he painted. Elsewhere, his relationship with the local and international art market is illustrated through works and documents. Thus, the Magritte Museum incorporates the components of a monograph, from biography to various ways of contextualizing the painter's life in his time. Paintings and documents, archives and films, photographs and drawings allow visitors to discover a world without imposing a discourse that congeals into a uniform interpretation. The narrative on the walls changes rhythm, and hence meaning, in step with the rehanging of the display and random encounters brought about by the arrival of a work on loan. This narrative is sketched out, suggested – never dictated in a one-dimensional way. Assembled from quotations, the texts by the painter that animate the exterior wall surface, blossom into a constellation – at times to find fault with the early avant-garde enthusiasm for the cult of progress and abstraction, at times to accompany what the paintings present to view in the progression of a thought.

This approach intersects with biography, which organizes the installation of the collection according to themes, each of which constitutes a viewpoint. The visit begins on the third level, which deals with abstraction, fashion and variety; the discovery of de Chirico; Surrealism's first steps in Belgium; photography as imagination; the 'word paintings'; and the Paris years. It is a sombre Magritte – of uniformly grey skies, haunted by the disturbing transformation of forms and the uncertainty of their future – whose paintings engage a reflection under the sign of the tormented psyche and diverted language. The second level presents the return to Brussels, the 'idiot' advertising work, the Brussels Surrealist group, portraiture, problematology, the struggle against Fascism and the war, 'Surrealism in Full Sunlight' and Communism, eroticism and the feminine ideal, the 'Vache' period and, finally, the first commercial successes with Iolas. By the end of this sequence, Magritte's work has assumed its final form, which is displayed on the last level in a different arrangement, under the sign of *The Enchanted Domain*. On this floor, the two large galleries that conclude the circuit are articulated around the dialogue that connects the works to each other. The intention is to show Magritte's painting as the workshop for an imagination that took shape on the threshold of the 1930s. Instead of limiting himself to restating what the gaze grasps in the instant of perception, the painter investigates the conditions of apprehension of a reality that eludes language in any form, visual or verbal. Executed late in 1932, *The Unexpected Answer* is one of the founding moments of the painter's career and leads in a straight line to the major works of the collection assembled at the end of the visit, from *The Domain of Arnheim* to *The Dominion of Light* and a number of masterpieces on loan or on deposit that deepen the dialogue, such as *Memory*, *The Heartstring*, *The Sixteenth of September*, *The Breast*, *The Art of Conversation* and *The Ignorant Fairy*. The groups composed open new perspectives that aim to enhance the perception of an œuvre and a way of thinking that lie at the heart of 20th-century art – an opening that relies on the organization of exhibitions focusing on particular questions. These exhibitions are the fruit of fundamental research carried out in connection with the Magritte Museum, so that in it, the painter's work finds not only a setting in which to be showcased but also a place in which to be perpetually reinvented.

Michel Draguet

Director, Royal Museums of Fine Arts of Belgium

– 1 –

BIOGRAPHY

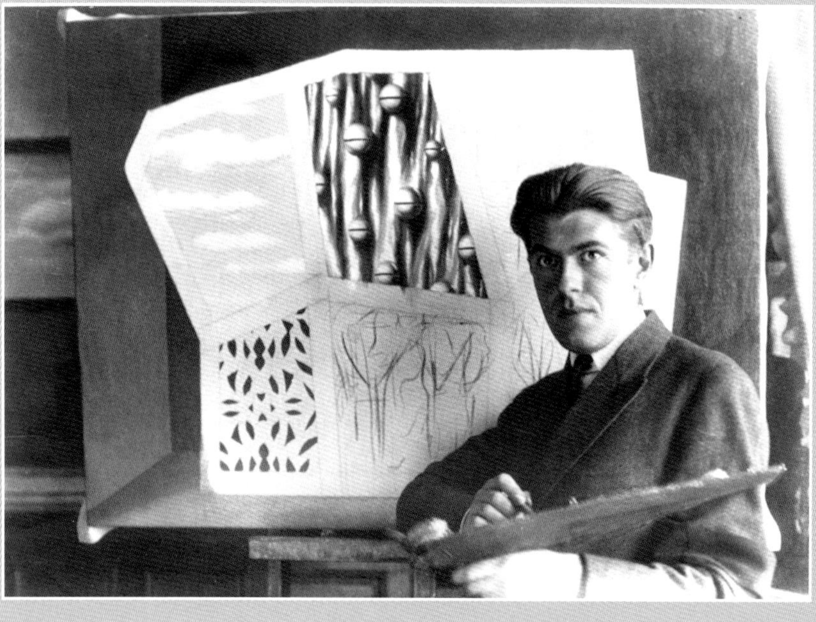

René Magritte with his palette in front of *The Empty Mask*,
Le Perreux-sur-Marne (Paris), 1928

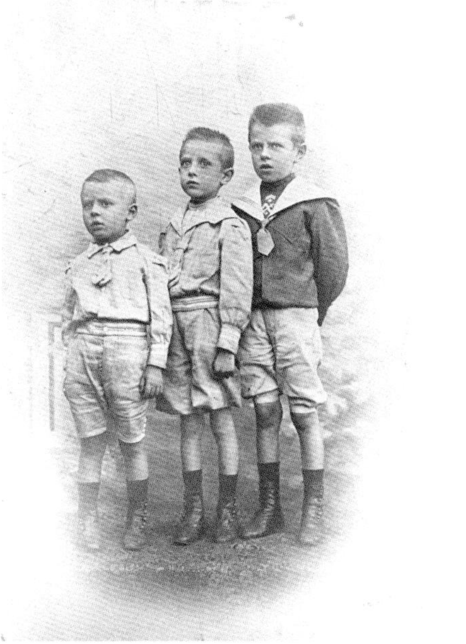
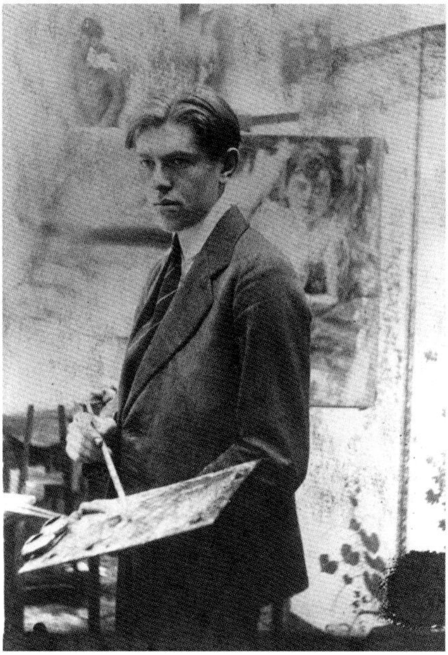

René Magritte was born in Lessines on 21 November 1898. As children, he and his two brothers were subjected to the upheaval of several moves and a tragic event, the suicide of their mother, who drowned herself in the River Sambre. Magritte began painting at school. At age seventeen, he left Charleroi, where he had met Georgette Berger, his future wife, and went to Brussels to begin studying at the Academy of Fine Arts. There, he met Victor Servranckx and Pierre-Louis Flouquet, with whom he discovered the contemporary art trends. At this time, Magritte began doing advertising work and created his first poster, for Pot au feu Derbaix (1918). He returned to this commercial activity sporadically throughout his life, whenever money was scarce. In 1920, he met E. L. T. Mesens, whose interest in Italian Futurism and Dada he shared. If Magritte was well acquainted with the art movements of his time and his paintings show the influences he underwent, everything changed in 1923, when his friend Marcel Lecomte showed him a reproduction of Giorgio de Chirico's *Song of Love* (1914). This revelation planted the seeds of his Surrealist work.

Paul, Raymond and René Magritte, 1905

René Magritte in the studio at the Academy of Fine Arts, Brussels, about 1918

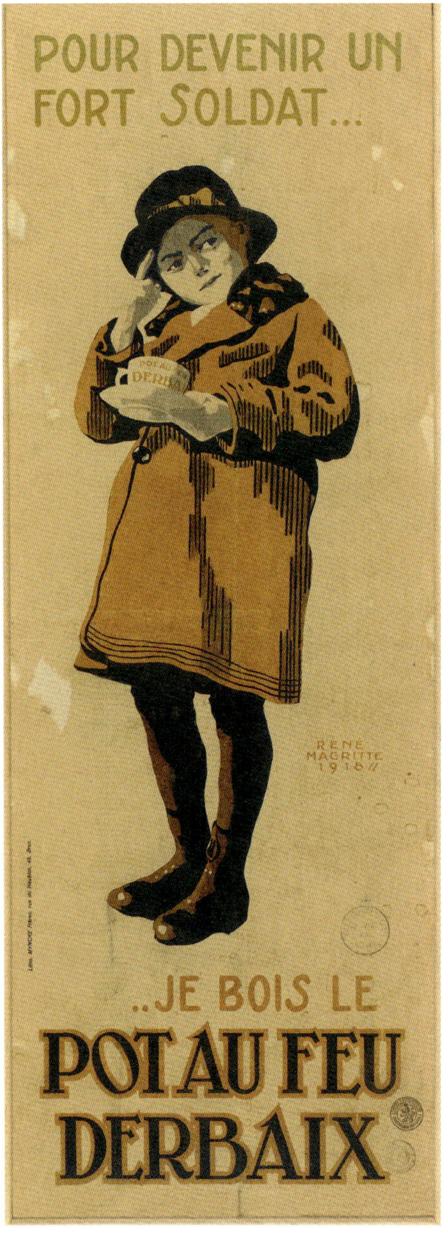

However, it was not until 1926, the year of the founding of the Belgian Surrealist group around Magritte, Mesens, Paul Nougé, Camille Goemans and André Souris, that he painted *The Lost Jockey*, considered to be his first Surrealist work. The following year, he exhibited sixty works in his first solo exhibition at the Centaure gallery, organized by Paul-Gustave van Hecke, his first dealer. From 1927 to 1930, the Magrittes lived in the Paris suburb of Perreux-sur-Marne. They took part in the activities of the French Surrealists and met Paul Eluard, André Breton, Joan Miró, Hans Arp and Salvador Dalí, among others. This period was important not only to Magritte's painting production (he painted more than a hundred works in 1928) but also to his theoretical views, for he published his famous text 'Words and Images' in *La Révolution surréaliste*, alongside the Parisians. In 1930, the Magrittes returned to Brussels because, in addition to the economic crisis, relations with Breton had become strained. Material difficulties forced Magritte to return to commercial art. With his brother Paul, he founded the advertising agency Studio

René Magritte
Pour devenir un fort soldat . . . je bois le pot au feu Derbaix
1918
Litho engraving on paper mounted on fibreboard
101 x 36.5 cm

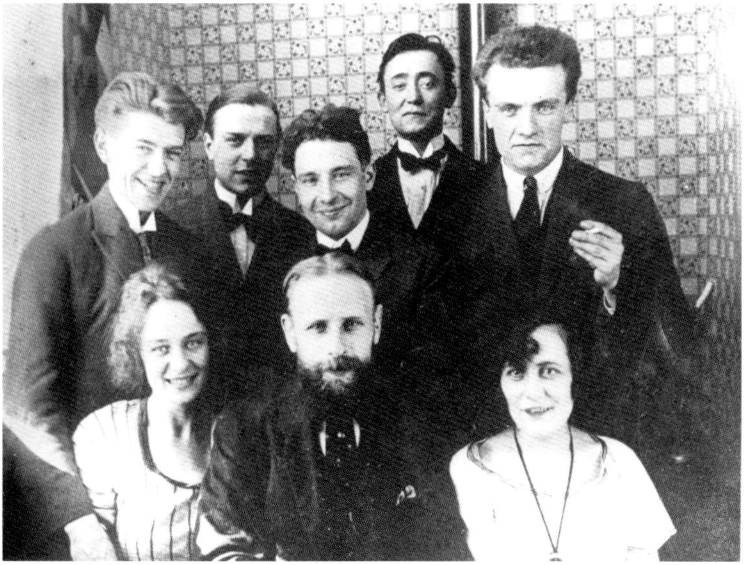

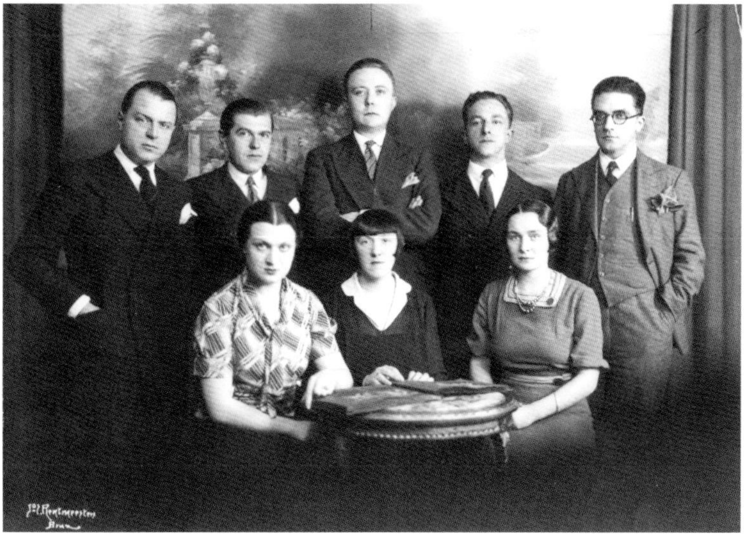

The 7 Arts group in Georgette and René Magritte's kitchen on their wedding day, Brussels, 28 June 1922
Left to right, standing: René Magritte, E. L. T. Mesens, Victor Servranckx, Pierre-Louis Flouquet, Pierre Bourgeois; seated: Georgette Magritte, Pierre Broodcoorens and Henriette Flouquet. A reproduction of the back of the photo bears the annotation: *At the Magrittes'. A gang of maniacs.* Brussels June '22

The hunting party, the Belgian Surrealist group, Brussels, 1934
Left to right, standing: E. L. T. Mesens, René Magritte, Louis Scutenaire, André Souris and Paul Nougé; seated: Irène Hamoir, Marthe Beauvoisin and Georgette Magritte

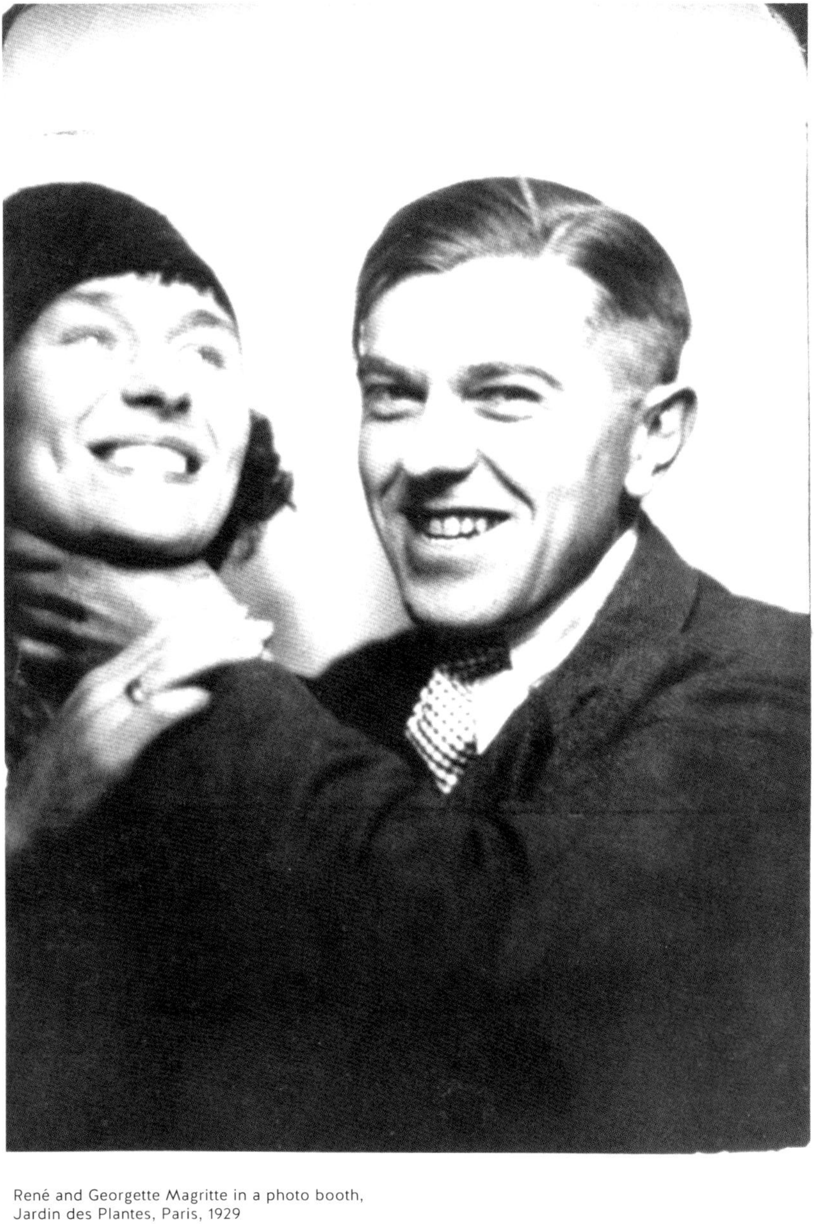

René and Georgette Magritte in a photo booth,
Jardin des Plantes, Paris, 1929

Dongo. During the 1930s, Magritte exhibitions were held abroad, in New York (1936 and 1938, Julien Levy Gallery), London (1938, London Gallery) and elsewhere. On the occasion of these first ventures into the international market, Magritte produced an abundance of works. He gradually entered into the logic that was to characterize the 1950s and 1960s. Buoyed by his success, he reproduced variants of his most appreciated works for an essentially American clientele. In 1938, Magritte gave a lecture entitled 'La Ligne de vie [Lifeline]', in which he recounted his past experiences and his artistic evolution – an evolution that took a sharp turn in 1943 when he initiated 'Surrealism in Full Sunlight', characterized by an Impressionist technique and a lightened palette. At the height of World War II, this ode to pleasure and the beautiful side of life offered an optimistic vision of the future. In 1948, Magritte hastily executed thirty paintings that were harshly criticized by Breton. His avowed aim was to make fun of the Parisians by sending these works of the 'Vache' period, as it is called, for his exhibition at the Galerie du Faubourg. The desire to break with French Surrealism coincided with Magritte's meeting Alexander Iolas,

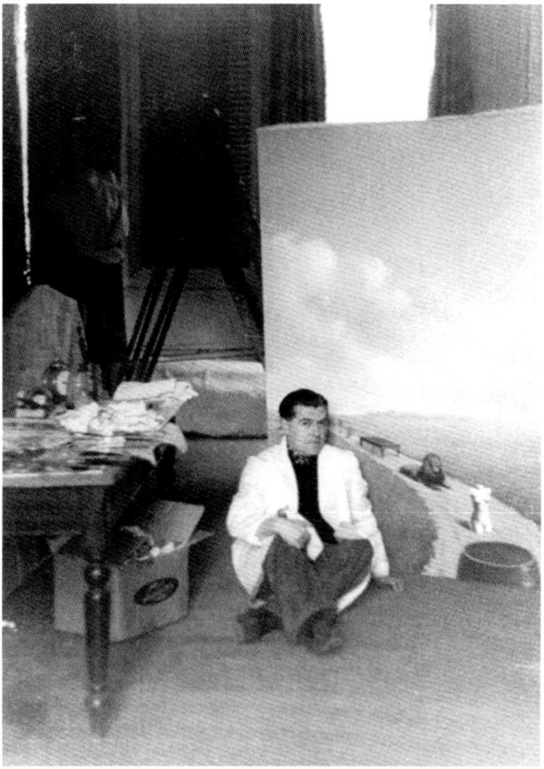

René Magritte in front of *Youth Illustrated*,
at Edward James's, Wimpole Street, London, March 1937

a key figure in the last twenty years of his life. Thanks to Iolas, who became his official dealer in the United States, Magritte achieved true success and began to make a living from his art. His works were then presented in solo exhibitions in Belgium and abroad, and he produced paintings for increasingly loyal collectors. In 1965, MoMA devoted a retrospective to him in New York, evidence of his importance on that side of the Atlantic. Two years later, Magritte died at home from cancer of the pancreas.

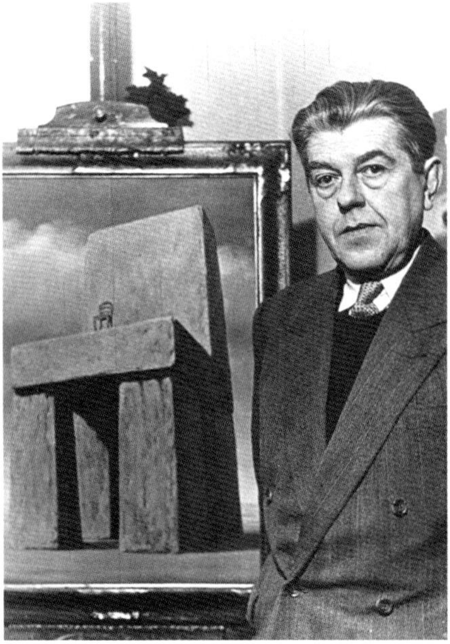

René Magritte in front of *The Legend of the Centuries*, 11 February 1953
Photo by Israël Shenker

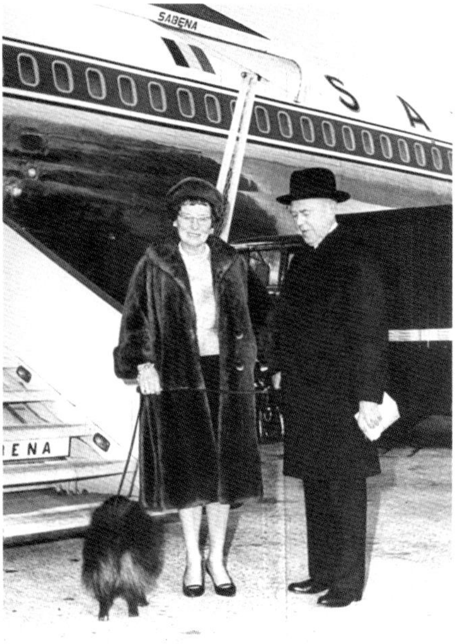

René and Georgette Magritte at Brussels airport before leaving for the United States, 8 December 1965

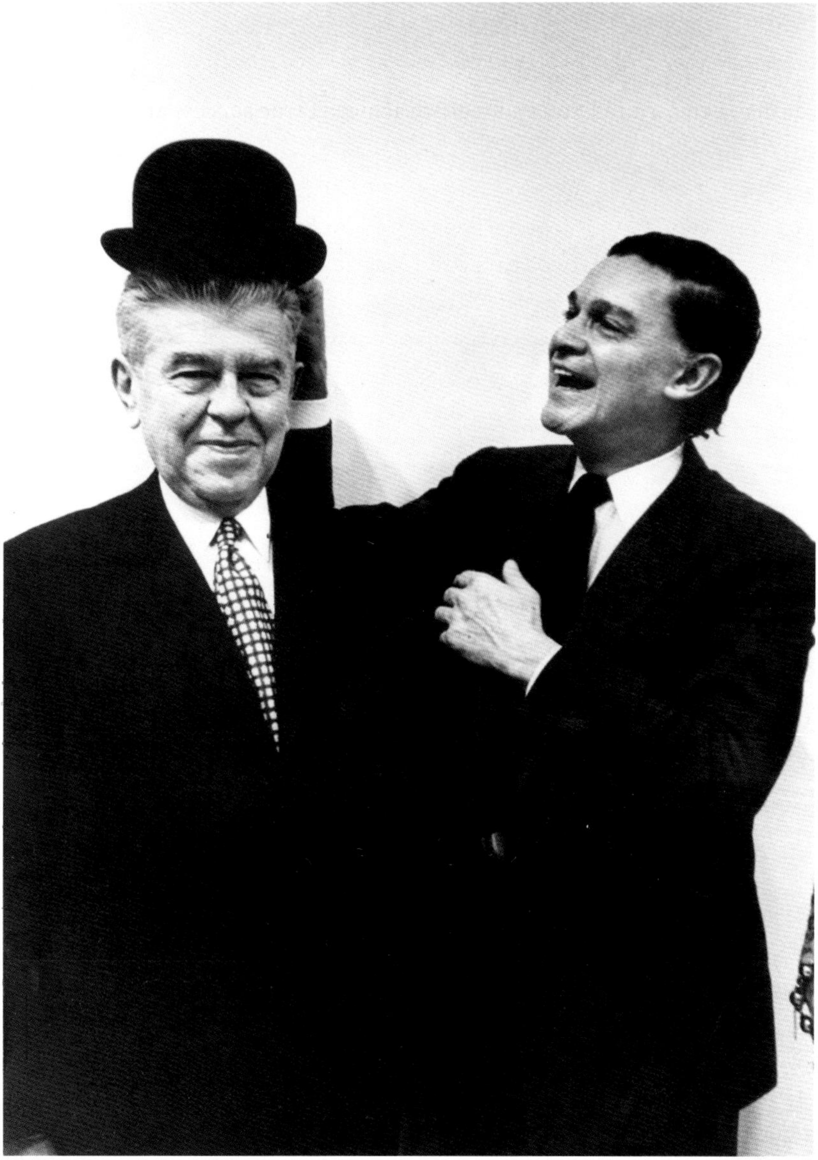

René Magritte and Alexander Iolas, 16 December 1965
Photo by Steve Schapiro

– 2 –

MASTERPIECES FROM THE COLLECTION OF THE ROYAL MUSEUMS OF FINE ARTS OF BELGIUM

This section includes thirty-one key works by René Magritte that belong to the collection of the Royal Museums of Fine Arts of Belgium. Presented chronologically, the selection reflects the circuit that visitors follow as they tour the museum. The explanatory entries aim to shed light on the works, which, in keeping with the spirit of Magritte, must however retain a share of mystery.

The Female Thief
Oil on canvas, 101 x 72.6 cm, 1927

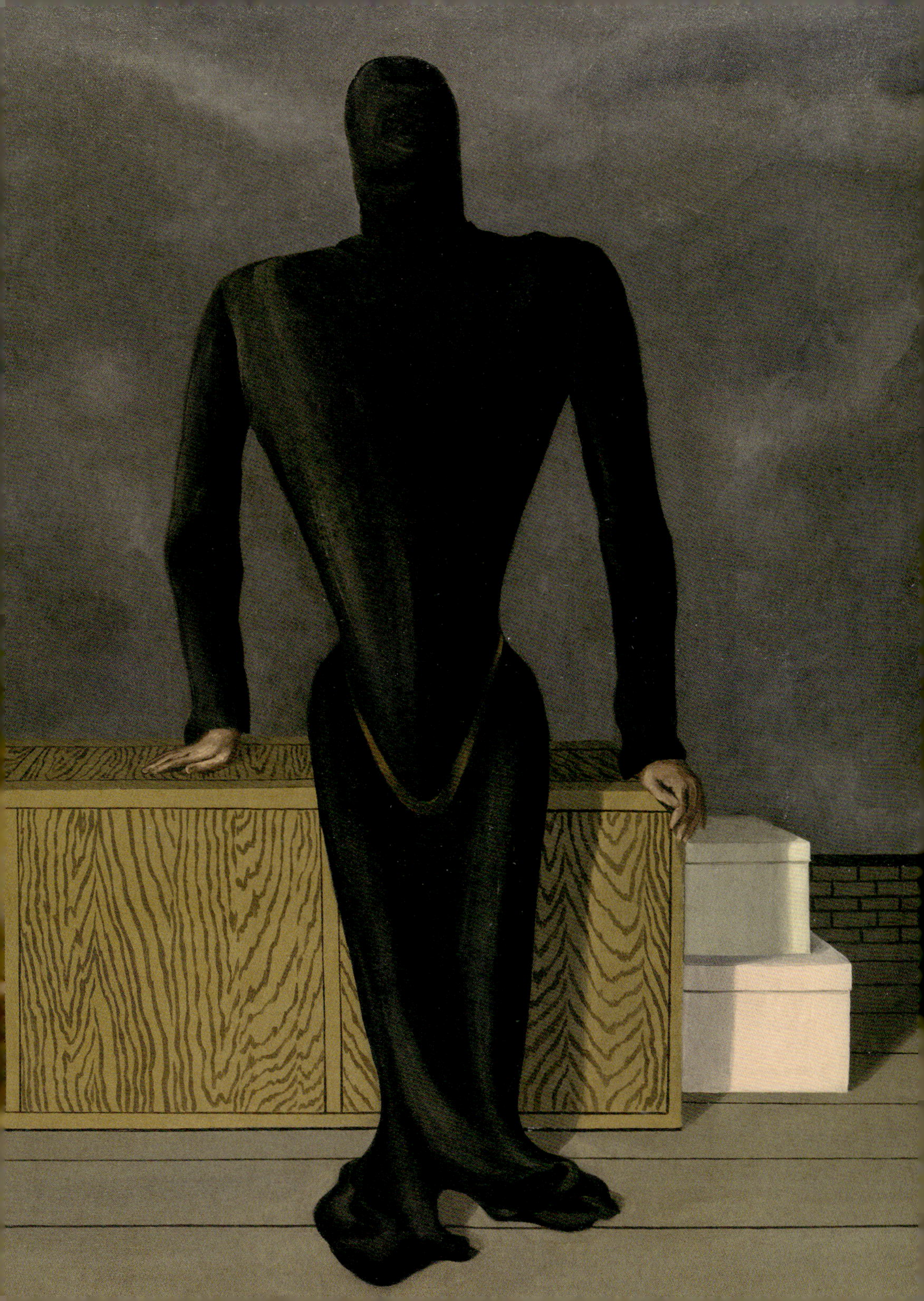

Woman on Horseback

1922
Oil on cardboard mounted on wood
63 x 90 cm
Inv. 12100

This painting from 1922 shows the influence of Cubism and Futurism on René Magritte at the beginning of his career. During his years at the Academy, he circulated in the art world, meeting famous personalities like Pierre and Victor Bourgeois, Pierre-Louis Flouquet, E. L. T. Mesens and Victor Servranckx. These companions of his early days introduced him to contemporary art movements like Cubism and Futurism. He procured a copy of Albert Gleizes's *Du cubisme et des moyens de le comprendre* (1920) and some Futurist exhibition catalogues. *Woman on Horseback* is an example of Magritte's art at a time when he was seeking his true path. He later called the works from this early phase 'evocative images, but abstract, inert and of interest only to the intelligence of the eyes'. In 1923, his art took a radical turn when he first saw *The Song of Love* by Giorgio de Chirico, 'the first painter to have thought of making a painting speak about something other than painting itself'. In tandem with his discovery of the collages of Max Ernst, who like de Chirico 'offered a new vision, where viewers find their isolation and hear the silence of the world', Magritte was preparing to launch into the adventure of Surrealism.

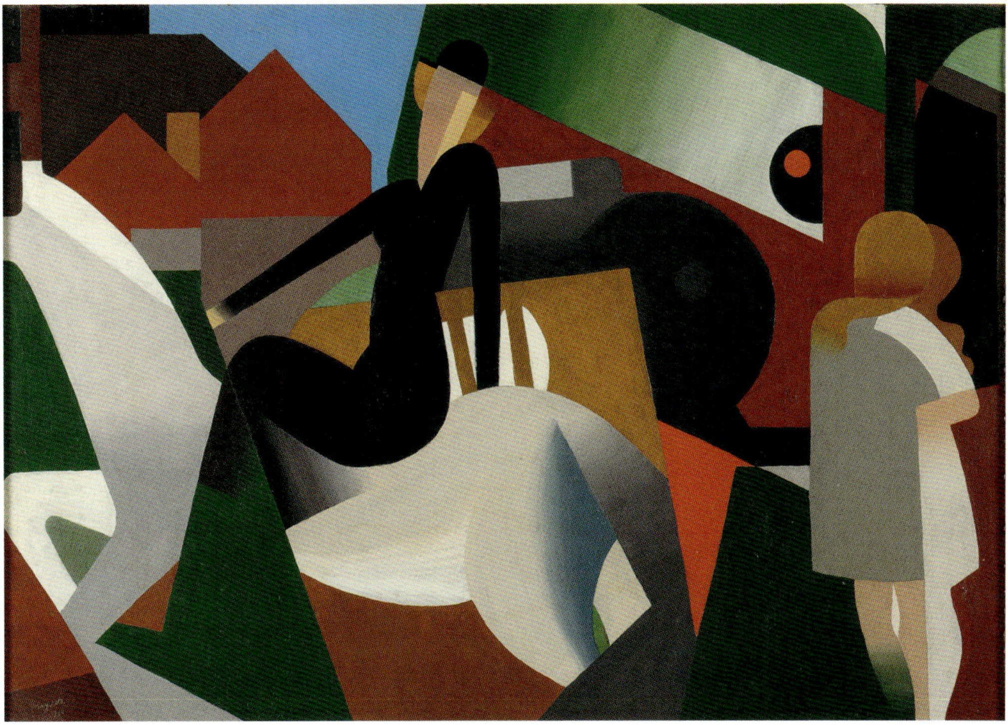

Primevère

1926
Litho engraving on paper
124 x 85.2 cm
Inv. 8584

René Magritte's art career is interspersed with what he later called 'idiot work'. At various times, Magritte worked for companies or individuals who commissioned posters and advertising drawings from him. Although at first he took an interest in such work, considering that it fuelled his imagination, it soon simply amounted to fulfilling a material necessity. In conjunction with his painting, this commercial activity allowed Magritte to develop a keen sense of the effective image needed for a successful advertisement. P*our devenir un fort soldat . . . Je bois le Pot au feu Derbaix* [To become a strong soldier . . . I drink Pot au feu Derbaix] is the first poster he made, in 1918 during World War I. Three years later, he was hired by Victor Servranckx at the Peters-Lacroix factory, where he created wallpaper patterns. Between 1924 and 1927, he worked for the fashion design firm Norine and then for the Brussels furrier Samuel designing a series of projects at first in a Cubist vein that prefigured his Surrealist compositions. When Magritte returned from Paris in 1930, he was unable to obtain work and founded Studio Dongo on Rue Esseghem in Jette with his brother Paul. This small firm carried out advertising campaigns: Paul secured the clients; Magritte made the drawings, posters, labels and various objects.

>>

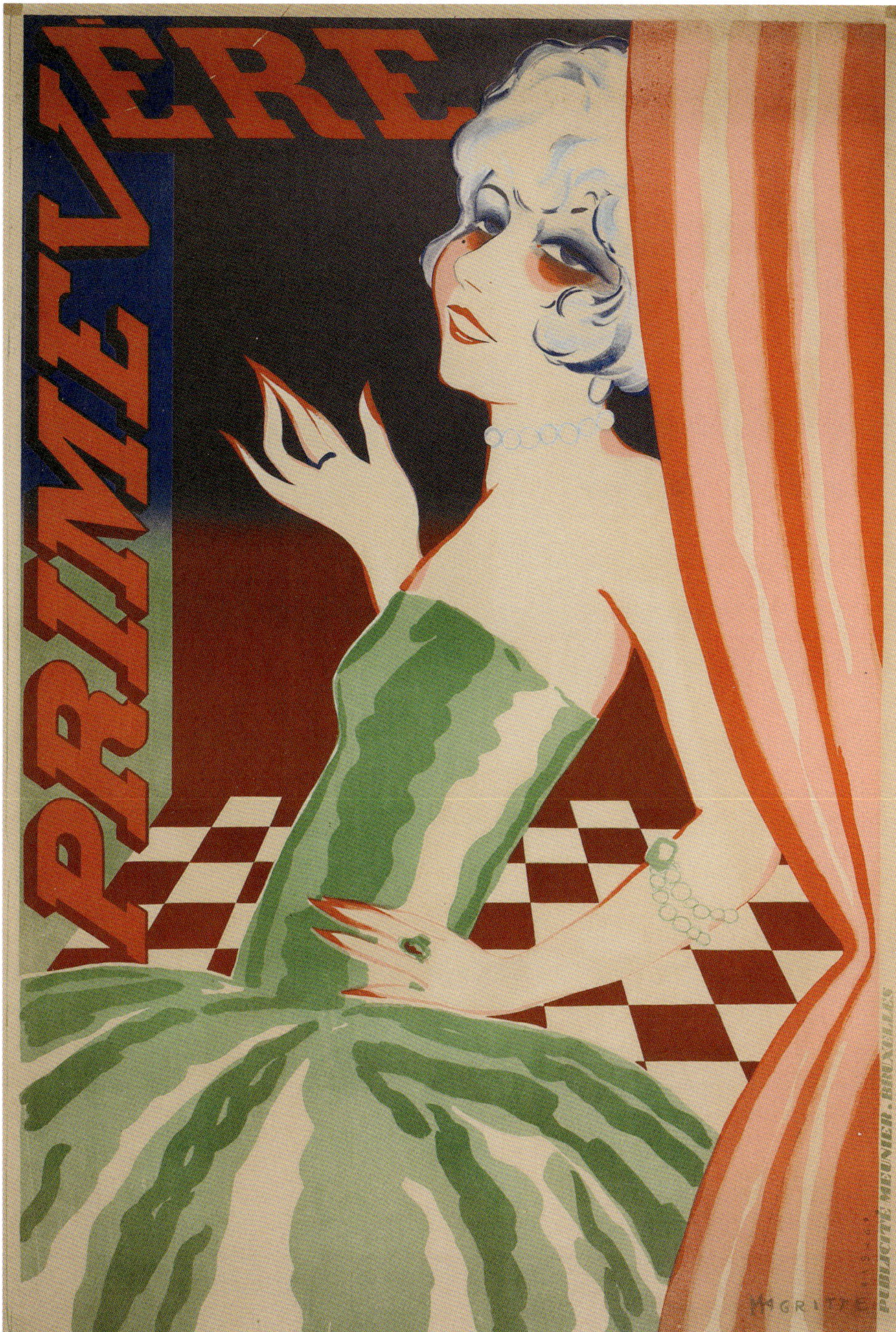
PRIMEVÈRE
MAGRITTE
PUBLICITÉ MEUNIER . BRUXELLES
LIT. FUYTINCK. BRUXELLES

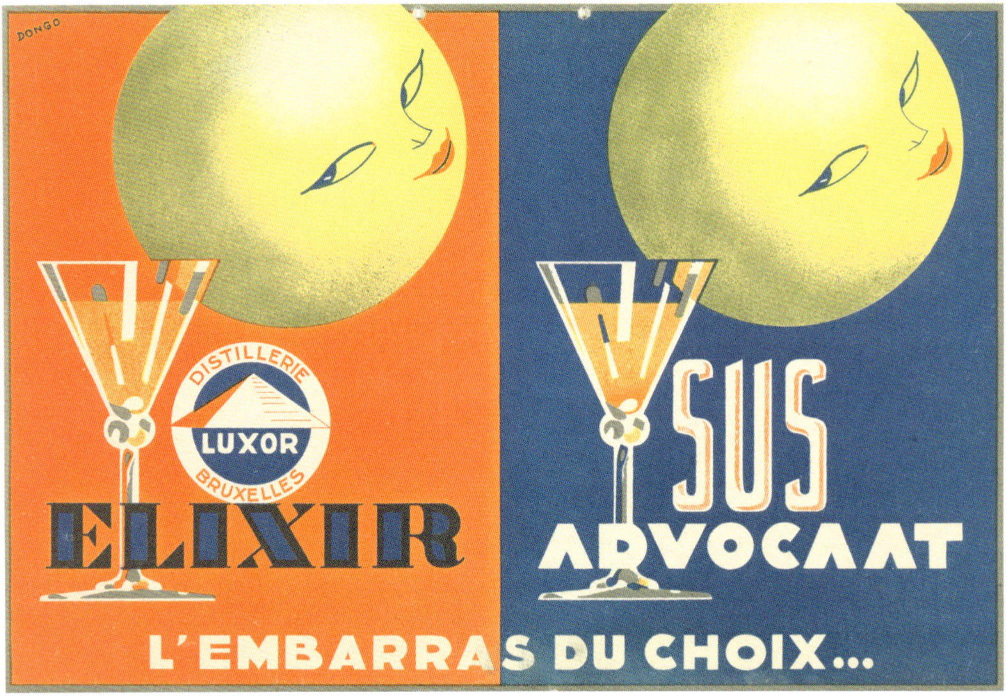
DONGO
DISTILLERIE
LUXOR
BRUXELLES
ELIXIR
SUS
ADVOCAAT
L'EMBARRAS DU CHOIX...

Distillerie Luxor, Bruxelles. Élixir. Sus. Advocaat. L'embarras du choix...

ca. 1936
Advertising panel, colour lithograph on paper
27.7 x 40.7 cm
Inv. 12314

In these conditions, he conceived the iconography of the poster *Distillerie Luxor*. It uses the device of the double, which he employed at various times in his paintings (for example nine years later in the *Portrait of Paul Nougé*). In his advertising work, Magritte put his imagination in the service of business by coming up with clever ideas or using elements from his paintings. In the poster *Primevère*, executed for an entertainer of that name, the curtain painted at the right of the composition to make the scene theatrical was to become a leitmotif in his paintings. Created in 1926, *Primevère* coincides with a turning point in Magritte's concept of the image, since he had decided 'from then on to paint objects only with their apparent details'. The realist aesthetic took shape, and the avant-garde forms disappeared.

SHEET MUSIC

In addition to advertising posters, Magritte designed nearly sixty-five sheet-music covers for Brussels and Paris publishers between 1924 and 1938. Among them are illustrations for music-hall numbers composed by his brother Paul, who founded Universal Star Edition. Magritte also received commissions from specialized publishers like Les Editions musicales de l'Art belge and Editions modernes. He signed these scores successively with the pseudonyms 'Magrit', 'Magritte', 'Dongo' and 'Emair'. The original drawings, which might be in any medium (charcoal, pastel, watercolour, gouache, etc.), were reproduced by the process of zincography, which had existed since 1850. The style of Magritte's illustrations is very graphic, and his representations reflect the contemporary period of the Roaring Twenties. The 1920s and 1930s saw a fundamental change in women's fashion: long, thin figure in a clinging dress; short hair, sometimes under a bonnet or a cloche; lipstick. Such was the often androgynous look of the modern emancipated woman, as depicted by Magritte in *Elle a mis son smoking* [She Was Wearing Tails] (1926). The practice of illustrating sheet music was widespread among young artists at the time. Magritte's friend and contemporary Pierre-Louis Flouquet also turned his hand to it.

Norine blues, vocal sheet music, illustrated by René Magritte; Musical Office, Brussels, 1925

Cinq mélodies orientales, sheet music for voice and piano, illustrated by René Magritte; Editions musicales de l'Art belge, Brussels, 1925

Elle a mis son smoking, sheet music for voice and piano, illustrated by René Magritte; Editions musicales de l'Art belge, Brussels, 1926

Mes rêves, sheet music for voice and piano, illustrated by René Magritte; Editions musicales de l'Art belge, Brussels, 1926

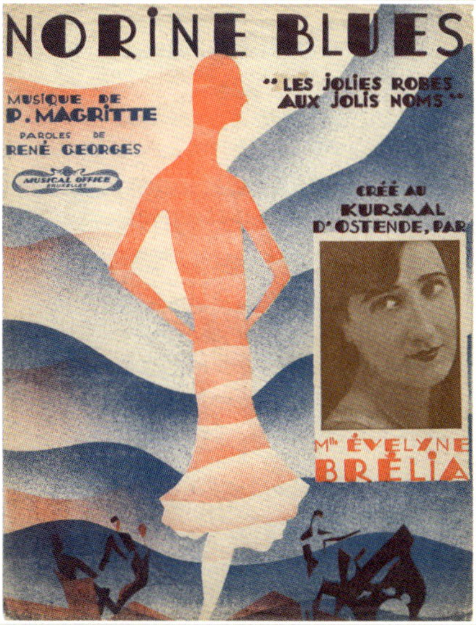
NORINE BLUES
MUSIQUE DE
P. MAGRITTE
PAROLES DE
RENÉ GEORGES
MUSICAL OFFICE
"LES JOLIES ROBES AUX JOLIS NOMS"
CRÉÉ AU KURSAAL D'OSTENDE, PAR
Mlle ÉVELYNE BRÉLIA

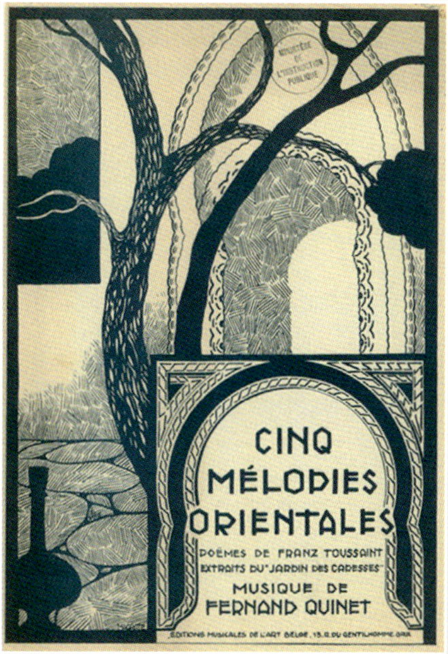
CINQ MÉLODIES ORIENTALES
POÈMES DE FRANZ TOUSSAINT
EXTRAITS DU "JARDIN DES CARESSES"
MUSIQUE DE
FERNAND QUINET

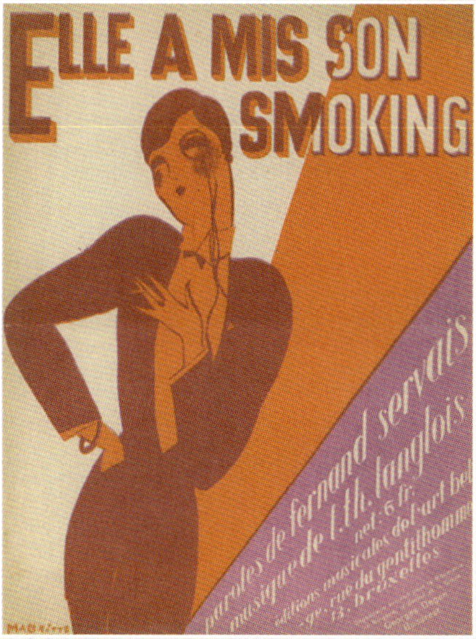
ELLE A MIS SON SMOKING
paroles de fernand servais
musique de l. th. langlois
net: 6 fr.
éditions musicales de l'art belge
-9- rue du gentilhomme
13. bruxelles

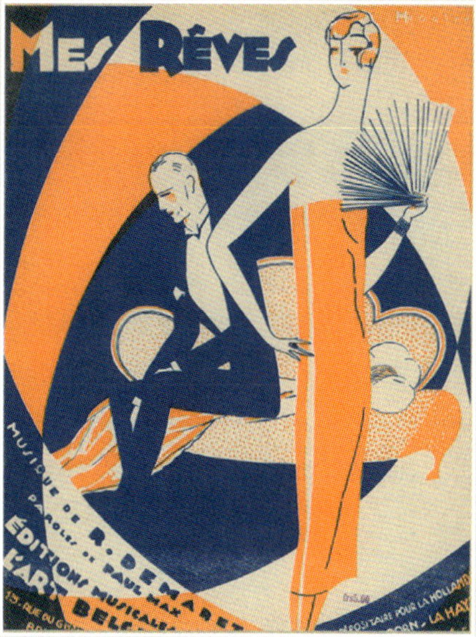
MES RÊVES
MUSIQUE DE R. DEMARET
PAROLES DE PAUL MAX
ÉDITIONS MUSICALES
L'ART BELGE

THE MIDNIGHT MARRIAGE

1926
Oil on canvas
139.5 x 105.5 cm
Inv. 7573

The Midnight Marriage is one of René Magritte's first Surrealist works. Fascinated by his discovery of the art of Giorgio de Chirico three years earlier, Magritte evoked the dreamlike and theatrical atmosphere he sensed when looking at de Chirico's *Song of Love*. If, in his Cubist and Futurist years, his main goal had been aesthetic, all that mattered now was the idea. Realistic rendering and smooth brushwork were essential to achieving Magritte's purpose of disorienting the viewer, of instilling uneasiness and perplexity. Several elements contribute to this reaction. The strange, pliant, almost organic masonry that structures the composition without indicating an interior or an exterior could refer to an episode Magritte recounted in 1962: 'I felt a vivid astonishment in looking from my cradle at some men who were removing a deflated balloon that had fallen on the roof of my parents' house.' This vision could be the source of the pliant forms that appear in his works starting in 1926. There are other disturbing elements as well: the trees in the background are growing upside-down; the mirror resting on the ground reflects only a shadow. But the two heads provide the main source of mystery. One is seen from behind, the other from the front, but neither face is visible. This closely guarded secret lies at the heart of Magritte's work and recurs in other compositions. In the mid-1930s, he invoked an extremely radical ban with *The Pleasure Principle*, where the face evanesces into nothing but a source of light. The poetry and mystery that emanate from *The Midnight Marriage* are what Magritte sought from this point on, 'an ever more striking, unexpected effect'.

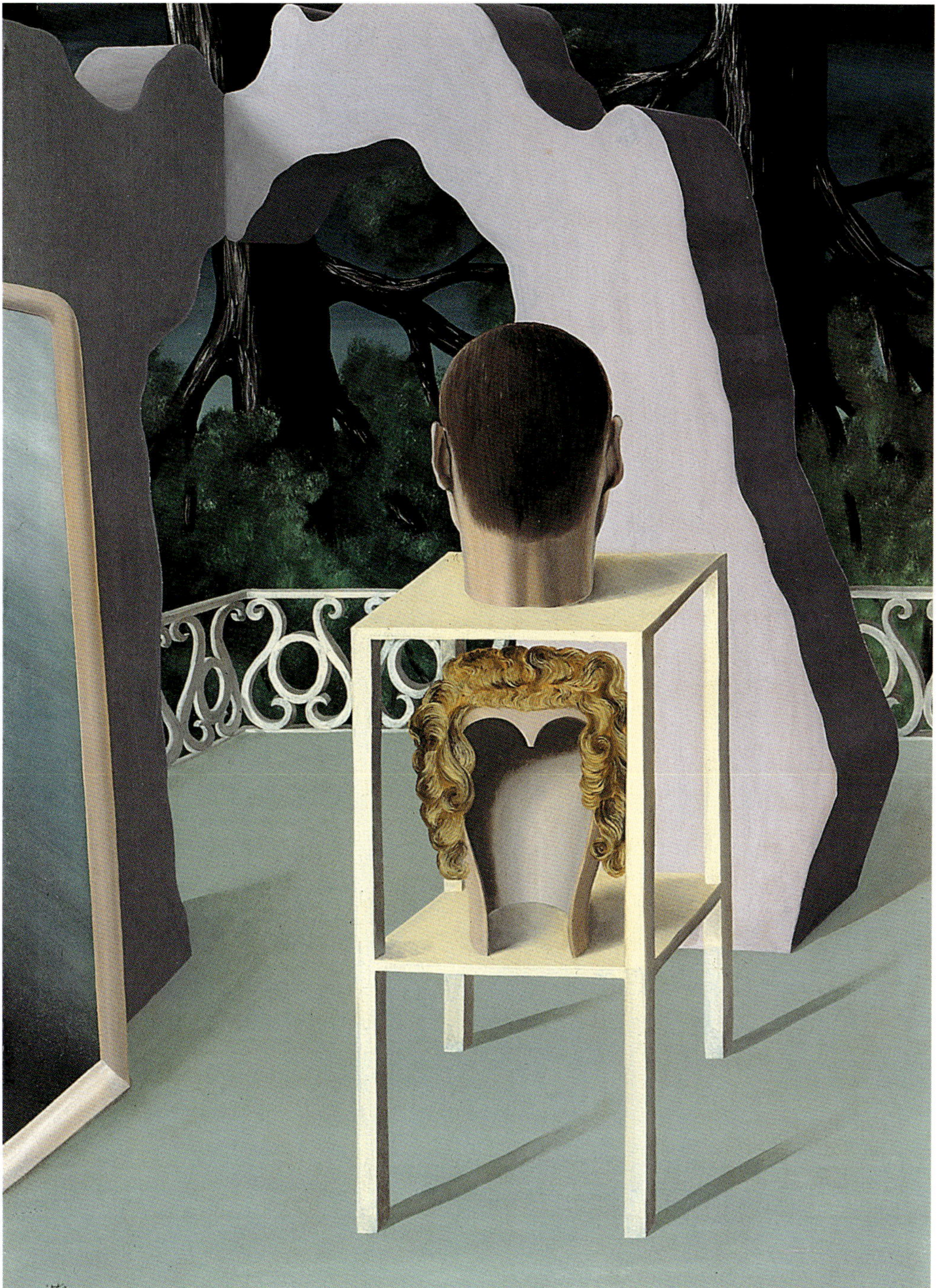
Magritte

The Man from the Sea

1927
Oil on canvas
139 x 105 cm
Inv. 7221

The Man from the Sea was given its title by Marcel Lecomte, a Surrealist poet and friend of Magritte. It refers to a film directed by Marcel L'Herbier in 1920 that tells the tragic tale of a sailor. The sombre, disturbing atmosphere and the feeling of fear that can emanate from this canvas are characteristic of Magritte's 'Dark' or, as he himself referred to it, 'Cavernous' period, which lasted from 1925 to 1930. This key work is also an allusion to Fantômas, a character created by Pierre Souvestre and Marcel Allain in 1911. The adventures of this hardened criminal, which Magritte had particularly enjoyed since his youth, were the subject of several films directed by Louis Feuillade. Magritte, a fan of this type of movie, offers up a reinterpretation of the final scene of *Juve against Fantômas*, in which a man in black prevails by setting off an explosion with the pull of a lever. While an air of mystery surrounds this man who looks like an Egyptian god, the painting attests above all to Magritte's use of references from the popular movies and novels that delighted him and inspired him throughout his career. Furthermore, this man from the sea's face remains as unknown as those in *The Midnight Marriage*. Transformed into a piece of wood, as in *The Conqueror*, painted the year before, it is another example of the important role of the face in Magritte's Surrealist work.

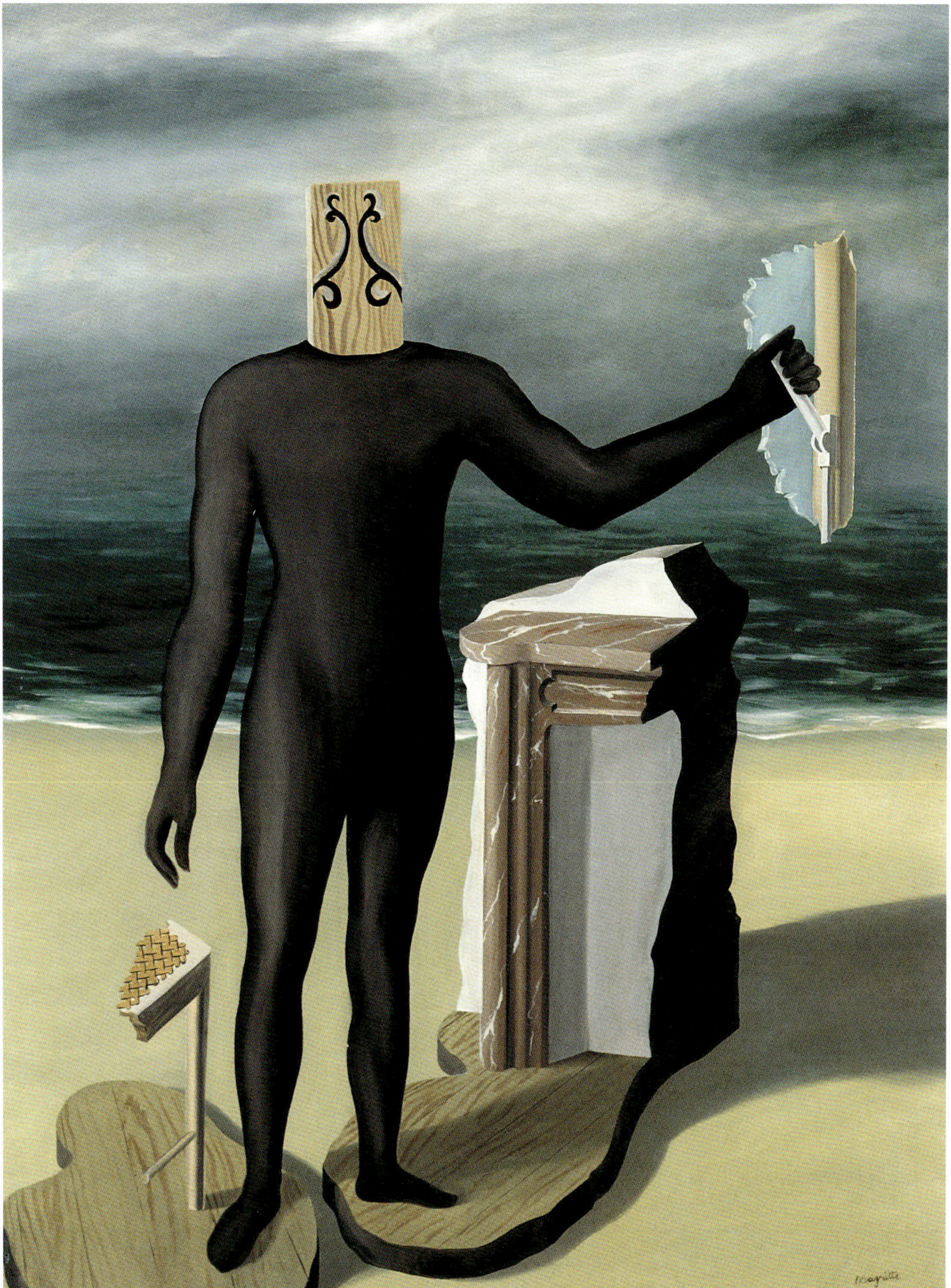

THE SECRET PLAYER

1927
Oil on canvas
152 x 195 cm
Inv. 11631

Along with *The Menaced Assassin* (MoMA, New York), *The Secret Player* forms a sort of diptych painted by Magritte in 1927 on two canvases of identical dimensions. These two works, the largest the artist ever painted, were exhibited together at Magritte's first solo show at the Centaure gallery in Brussels that year. As with the poster *Primevère*, Magritte placed a red curtain at the right to suggest a stage. Viewers attend a performance that is taking place before their eyes, but whose meaning they do not grasp. A similar composition was depicted a year later in *The Lost Jockey*, considered to be Magritte's first Surrealist work. Contrary to the issues presented in *Woman on Horseback*, for example, 'He painted "The Lost Jockey", conceived with no concern for aesthetics, for the sole purpose of responding to a mysterious feeling, an anxiety "for no reason".' Magritte employed various devices here to achieve this result. First, the combination of elements that are recognizable individually but lose all logical meaning when considered as a whole. Next, giving life to inanimate objects, in this case bowling-pin trees with branches and flowers. And finally, the play on proportions, where the giant bowling pins towering over little athletes could allude to *Gulliver's Travels* by Jonathan Swift. In addition to the red curtain and the bowling pins, this large painting includes another of the painter's recurrent elements: the giant tortoise copied from the *Encyclopaedia Larousse* that appears in later works.

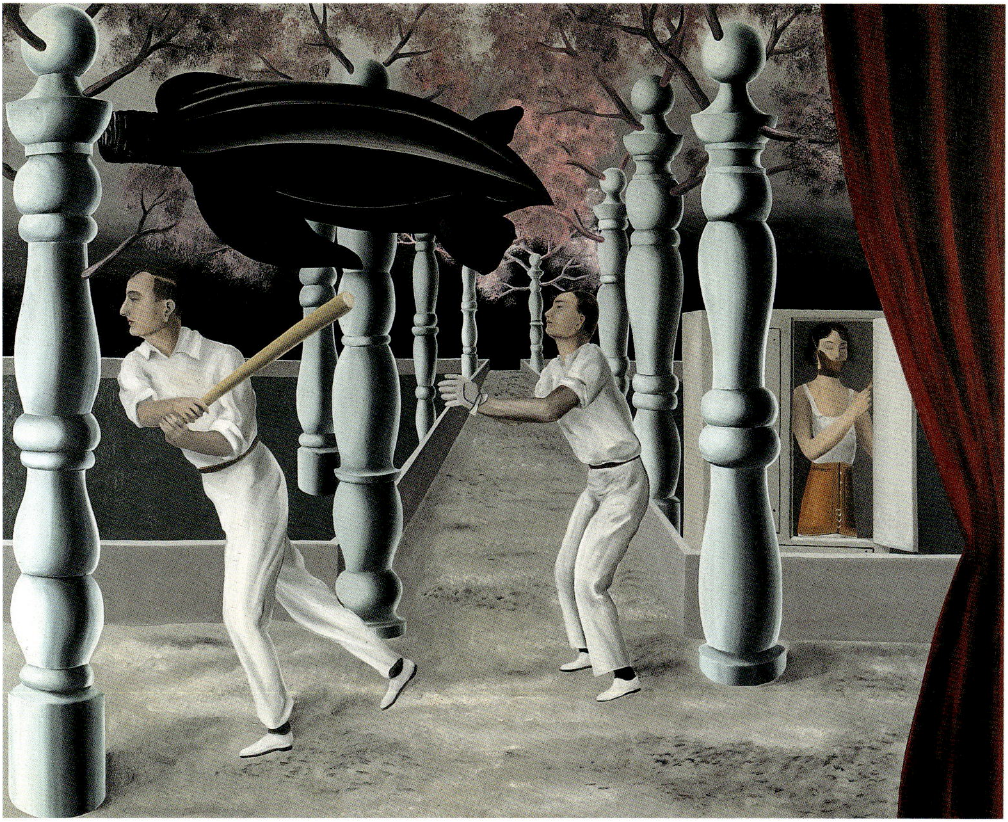

DISCOVERY

1927
Oil on canvas
65.2 x 50.3 cm
Inv. 11675

One of the methods Magritte developed to throw the viewer off balance is metamorphosis. In a letter of November 1927 to his friend and mentor the poet Paul Nougé, who would soon write *René Magritte, ou Les Images défendues* [René Magritte, or Forbidden Images], the painter explained, 'I believe I have made a discovery regarding painting that is quite striking: until now, I had been using composite objects, or else the positioning of an object was enough to make it mysterious. But subsequent to my research here, I have found a new possibility in things: to gradually become something else; an object blends into an object other than itself. For example, wood shows through in the sky in certain places. This, it seems to me, is something other than a composite object, since there is no rupture between the two materials, no dividing line. By this means I obtain paintings where the gaze "must think" in a completely different manner from usual; things are tangible, and yet some planks of good wood become imperceptibly transparent in certain places. Or else parts of a nude woman turn into a different material.' Magritte could have drawn his inspiration from various sources for this *Discovery* (originally entitled *L'Expérience du miracle* [Experiencing a Miracle]): a scene from Man Ray's film *Return to Reason* (1923), Fernand Khnopff's painting *The Caress* (1896) or perhaps a postcard depicting a woman in a similar pose.

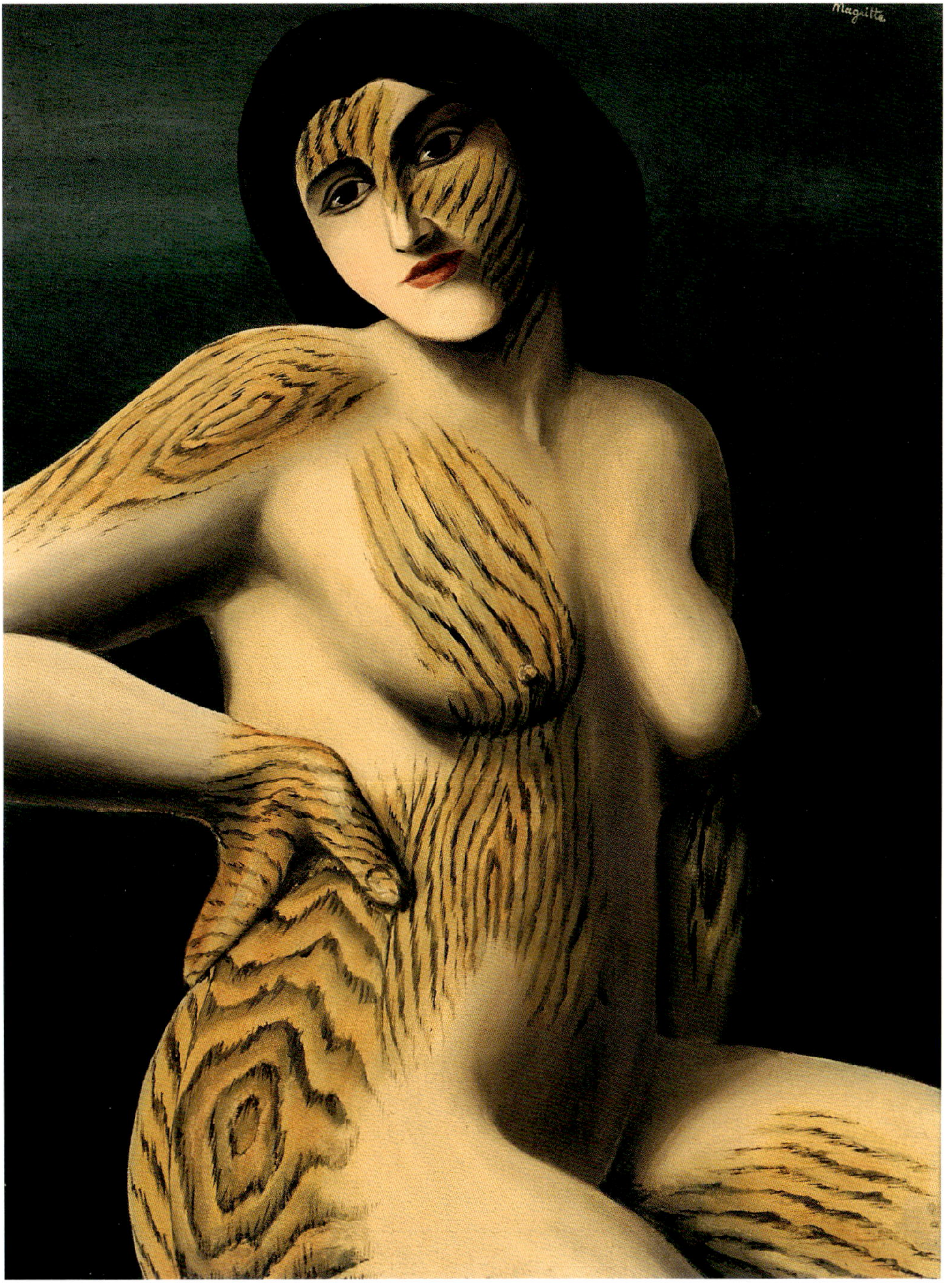
Magritte

Portrait of Paul Nougé

1927
Oil on canvas
94.3 x 64.5 cm
Inv. 11676

This is a double portrait of Magritte's friend Paul Nougé, a leader of Brussels Surrealism. Double representation is found at the same period in *Foolhardy* (1927), about which the artist explained, 'A person's appearance takes on a mysterious power when it is accompanied by his reflection,' adding, 'Alone, it does not evoke what it has in common with all beings, that is to say their mystery.' Dressed in tails (which in reality he never wore) and wearing glasses, Nougé strikes a serious pose in keeping with his incisive personality and E. L. T. Mesens's description of him as 'rigour personified'. He represented Surrealism's thinking mind and founded the journal *Correspondance* in 1924. Among the signers of its somewhat subversive pamphlets were Camille Goemans and Marcel Lecomte, two key players in Brussels Surrealism, which took form officially in 1926. They were joined by Magritte, Mesens, Nougé and Souris. The cell-like surface in the background recalls other works from the same period, like *The Blood of the World* (1927). Here, it may refer to Nougé's profession as a biochemist.

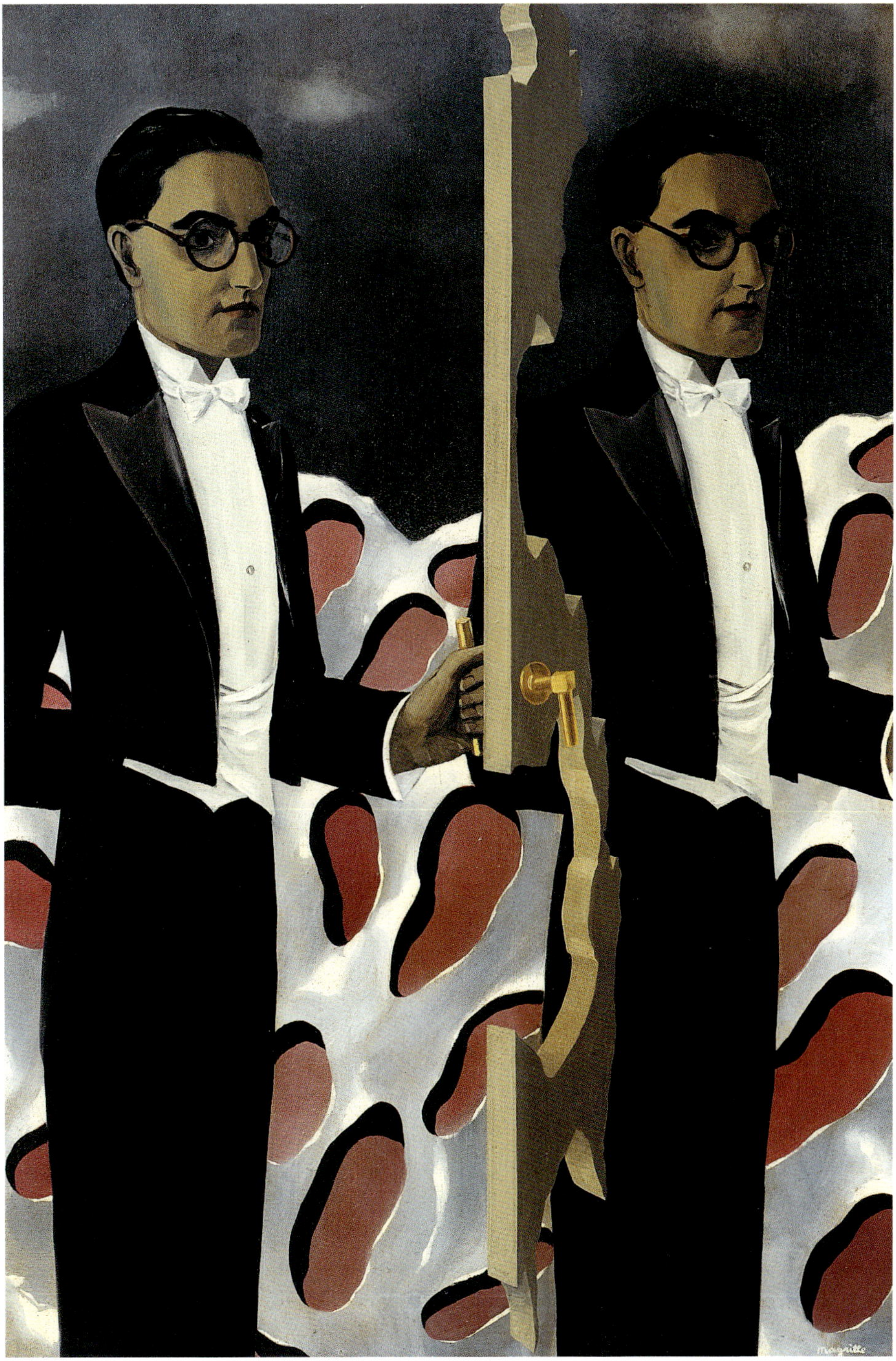
Magritte

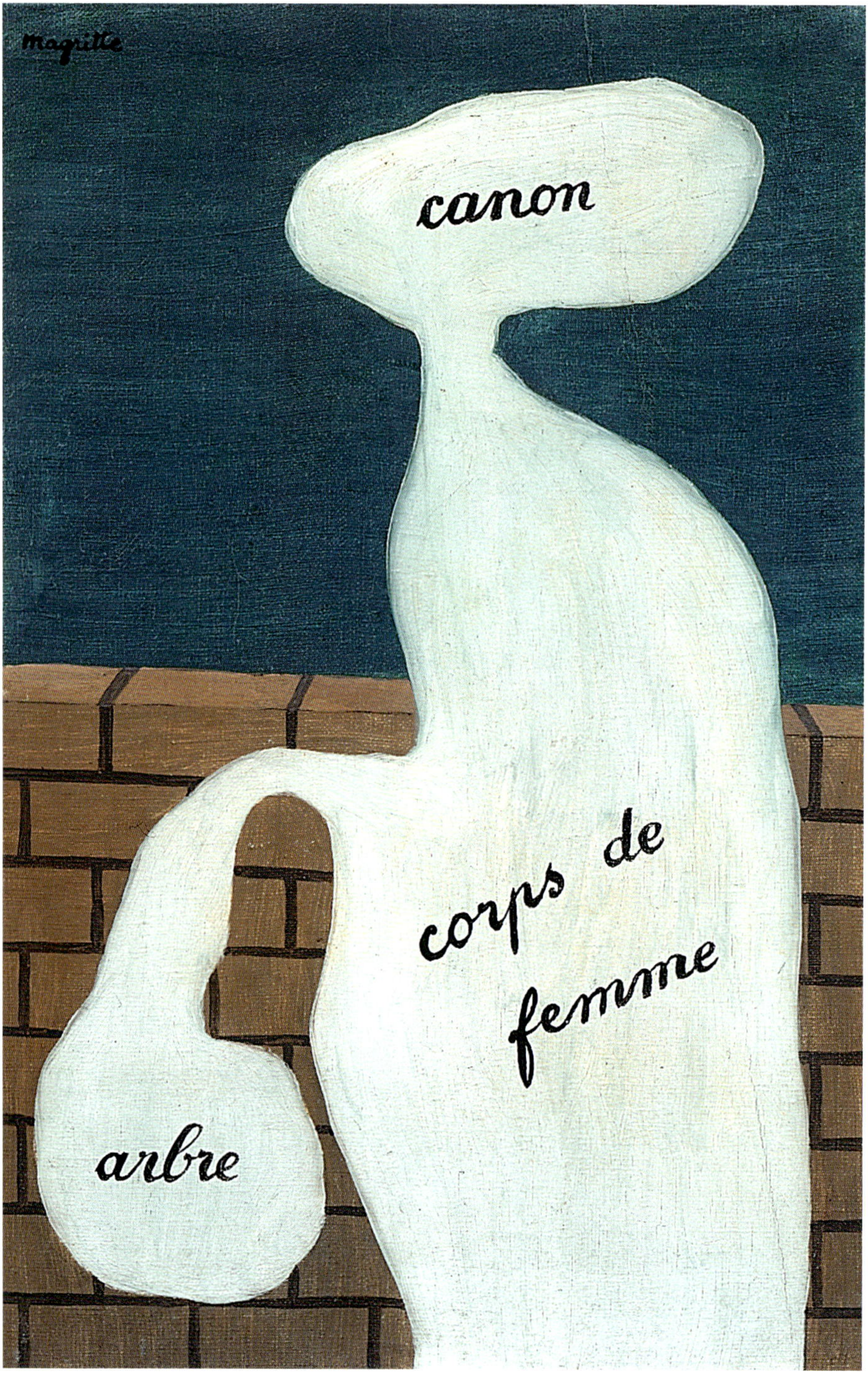

–40

The Use of Speech

1927-1929
Oil on canvas
41.8 x 27.3 cm
Inv. 11530

This canvas strongly recalls the series of 'word paintings', or 'alphabet paintings', that were the culmination of Magritte's Paris stay from 1927 to 1930. In his illustrated text 'Words and Images', published in 1929 in the twelfth and last issue of *La Révolution surréaliste*, Magritte set down eighteen aphorisms on the relationship between word and image. They emphasize the arbitrary link between an image and its denomination – between reality and its representation ('This is not a pipe') – and Magritte's mistrust of the role of communication ascribed to language. In this text, a sort of user's guide to reading the word paintings, there is an aphorism that applies perfectly to *The Use of Speech*, where the words are inscribed in indeterminate forms: 'Sometimes, the names written in a picture designate precise things, while the images are vague.' Of note in this regard is *The Treachery of Images* (1929) – among the best-known works from this period – in which 'everything tends to make one think there is little relationship between an object and what represents it'. And in fact 'this is not a pipe', but its representation, at times pictorial, at times scriptural. As Magritte pointed out, 'Who could smoke the pipe in my painting? No one.'
The best known of Magritte's writings, 'Words and Images' is a major contribution to 20th-century art.

FIGURE BROODING ON MADNESS

1928
Oil on canvas
54 x 73 cm
Inv. 11680

This strange work dates from the period when Magritte was developing his Surrealist vocabulary, but shows few characteristic features. A serious-looking man in profile points a finger in one direction, while his deep gaze is fixed on 'something' outside the frame. The table is white, and nothing in the picture gives any hint as to what the object of his attention might be. The viewer's imagination is called into play. This well-kept secret is related to the theme of the invisible and hidden, and promotes Magritte's desire to throw viewers off balance, to cause them to experience a kind of anxiety in the face of an impenetrable unknown. Although the title given by Paul Nougé might help viewers interpret this canvas, Magritte nonetheless insisted in 1938, in his famous lecture 'La Ligne de vie [Lifeline]', that 'Paul Nougé, in *Les Images défendues*, also notes that the titles of my paintings are fuel for conversation, not explanations. The titles are chosen to prevent anyone from locating my paintings in a reassuring region that the automatic progression of thought would find for them so as to undermine their impact.'

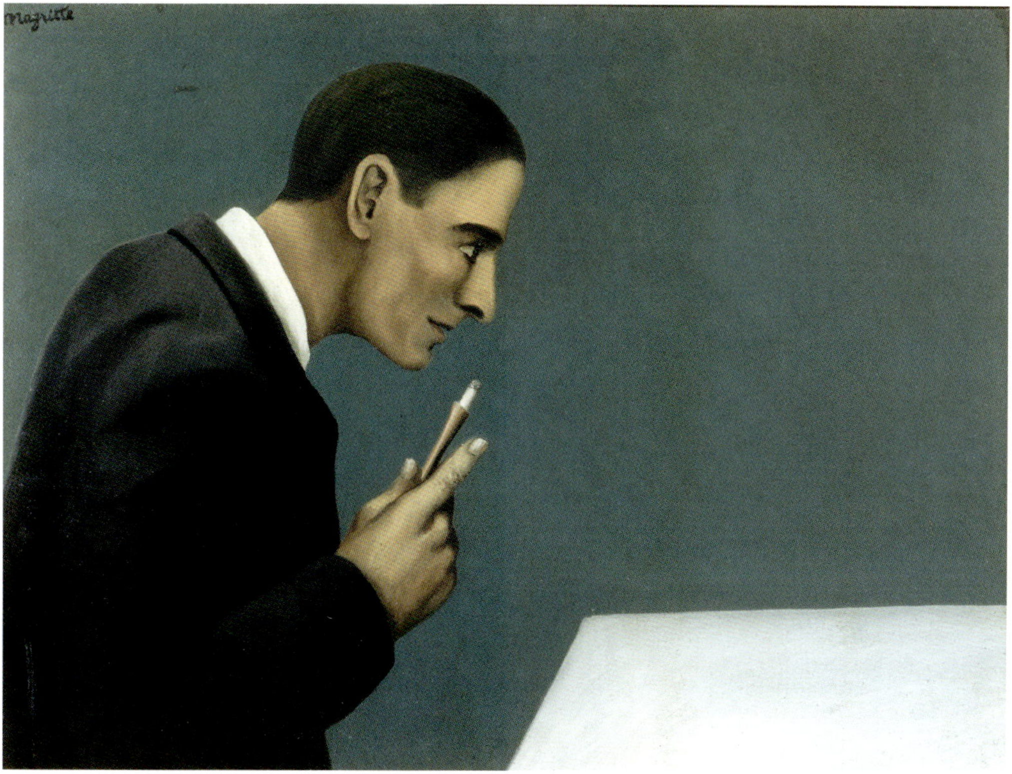

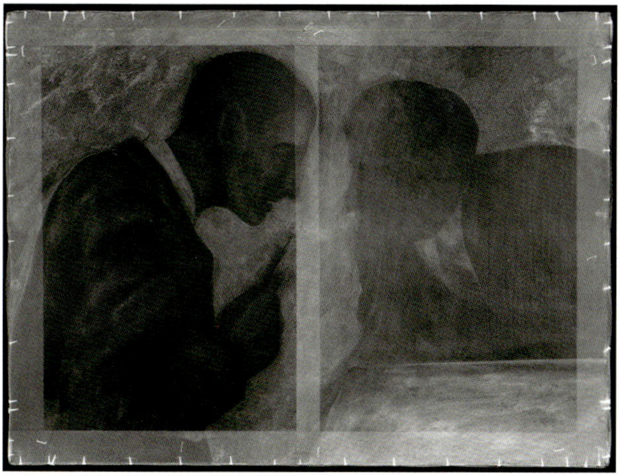

X-ray photograph:
The Royal Museums X-rayed this work in December 2012. Aimed at analysing a painting through imaging techniques, this procedure makes it possible to examine the underlying paint layer and detect overpainting, as well as provide data essential for preventive conservation. The X-ray of this canvas revealed a radical change in the composition initially conceived by Magritte, exposing a second figure. The study of other works dating from Magritte's early Surrealist period indicates the same phenomenon and could lead to a reconsideration of the painter's work methods and the evolution of his compositions.

The Imp of the Perverse

1928
Oil on canvas
81.3 x 116 cm
Inv. 7418

The Imp of the Perverse is from a series of paintings undertaken in 1927 that share the same concept: a metallic surface with a biomorphic contour is pierced with openings, some empty, some filled in with sky or wooden boards. What is peculiar to this canvas is its background. The irregular form is not set vertically on a floor (*The Lightbreaker*) or dark terrain (*The Travel Season*), but seems to float above the ocean. The motion of the waves is rendered with thickly applied paint – a rarity in Magritte's technique. This detail is all the more remarkable in that it contrasts with the smooth surface of the floating form. The artist uses impasto as if to dramatize the scene. This canvas's unexpected composition and strange atmosphere are among the most mysterious in Magritte's œuvre, exemplifying his idea that 'art should evoke the mystery without which the world would not exist'. This reference to the sea against a background of dark sky and the particular shape chosen by Magritte could refer to Arnold Böcklin's *Isle of the Dead* (1880), a painting greatly admired by the Surrealists. The title, which prevents the viewer from 'locating the painting in a reassuring region', is taken from a tale by Edgar Allan Poe, one of the artist's favourite authors.

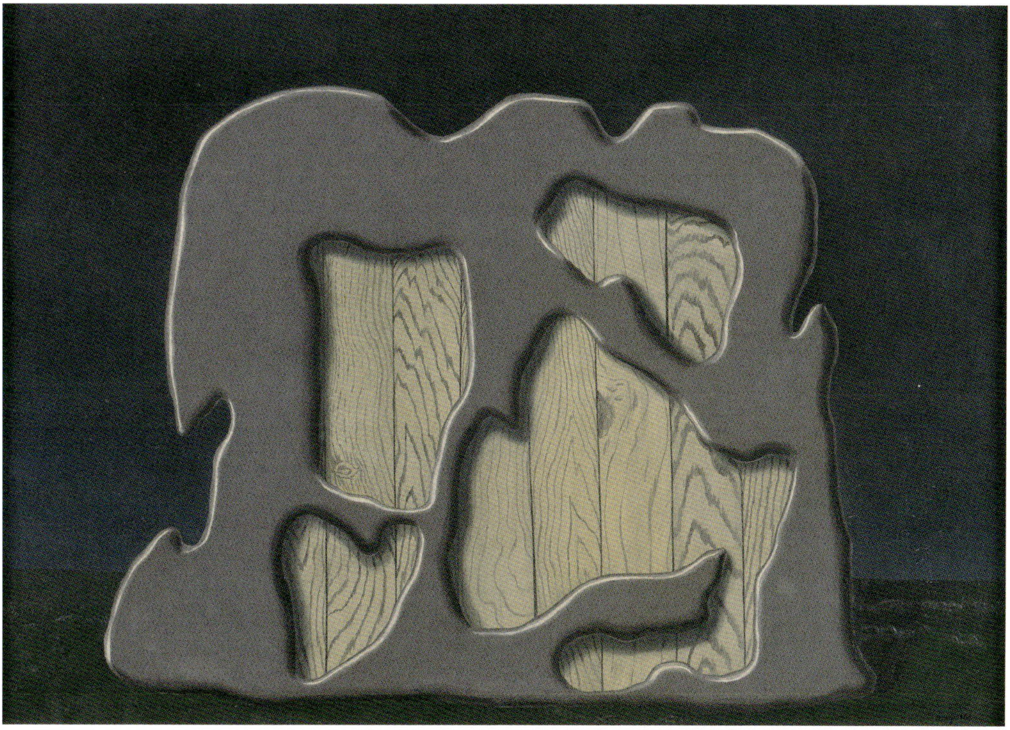

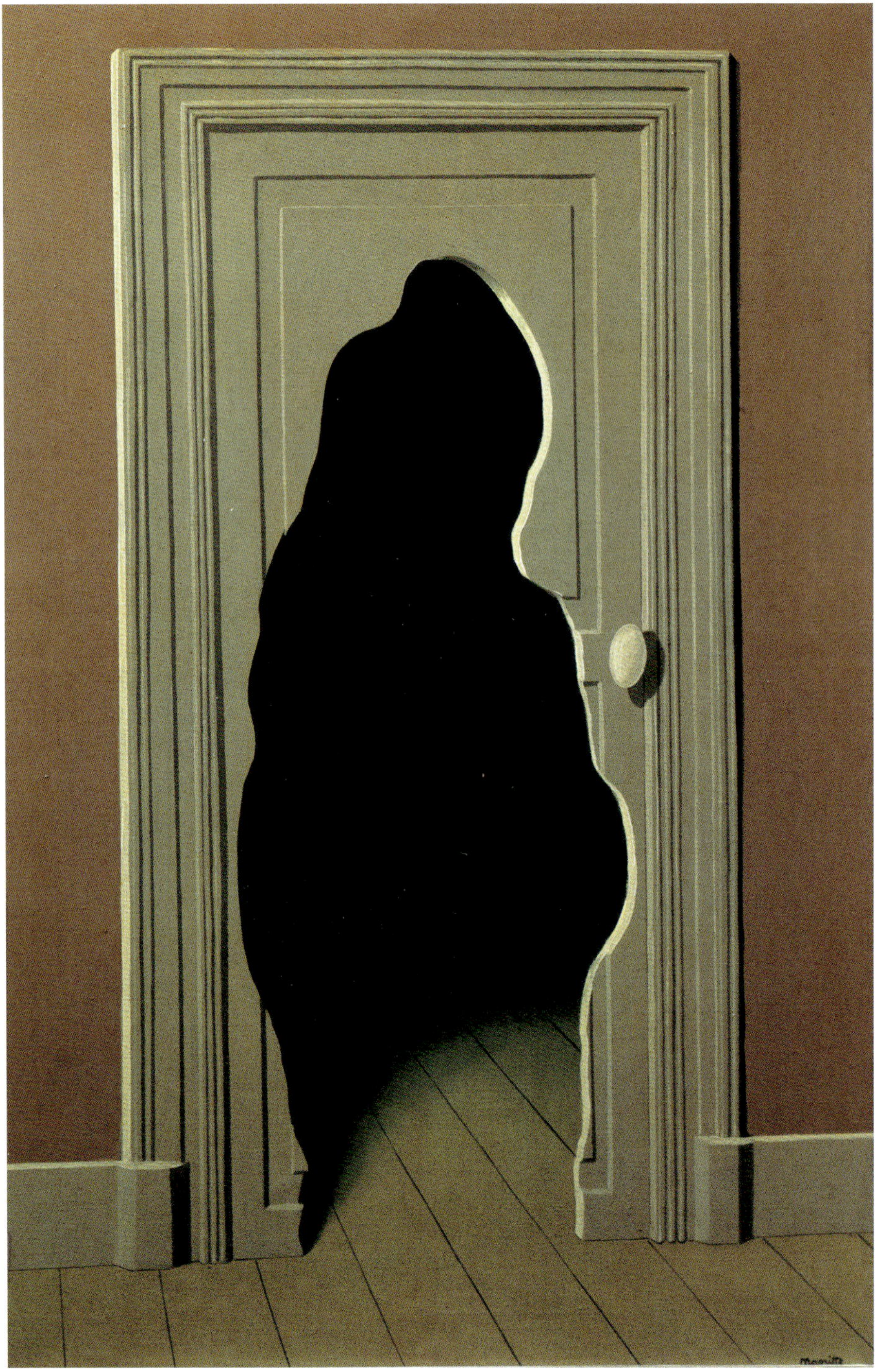

–46

THE UNEXPECTED ANSWER

1932
Oil on canvas
82 x 54.4 cm
Inv. 7241

Surrealism's major contribution may be the chance it offers viewers to rediscover the everyday objects around them. These objects, which have become invisible from over-familiarity, regain all their meaning with Magritte. A great number of works by the painter present 'disturbing poetic realities', and their success is due to their capacity to perturb the viewer and provoke perplexity and reflection. In 1932, after Magritte had returned to Brussels, his work adopted new pictorial perspectives. The idea then became to combine objects and concepts connected through predestination, their juxtaposition making it possible to draw attention to something obvious that had been forgotten – some original meaning attached to the object and buried in the unconscious. This principle of 'elective affinities' (which is also the title of a painting depicting an egg in a cage) arose from these surprising juxtapositions of subjects that maintain inextricable relationships to be *rediscovered*. In 1947, Magritte's perennial friend Louis Scutenaire said of *The Unexpected Answer*, 'Everyday things – slippers, egg, door – become so familiar that over time they lapse into invisibility. But Magritte drags these objects back from the void and slowly the world is repopulated . . . After all, the *raison d'être* of the door is not to be rectangular and made of wood, but, if I may say so, to let us pass through it. Let the painter put an opening in it, and the obvious bursts forth: the door regains the meaning it lost . . . And we are far from the gratuitous misleaders who, using a door, close it in our face.' For Magritte, 'the problem of the door called for an opening one could pass through'. He found the solution in painting *The Unexpected Answer* – a gaping hole in a closed door.

EXQUISITE CORPSE

'*Exquisite Corpse.* – A game with folded paper in which a sentence or drawing is composed by several players without any of them being aware of the previous contribution or contributions. The classic example, which gave the game its name, is the first sentence derived in this manner: "The exquisite – corpse – will drink – the new – wine."' This definition appeared in the *Abridged Dictionary of Surrealism*, published in French in 1938 by André Breton and Paul Eluard. In 1925, the artists in the circle of Marcel Duhamel had begun playing Exquisite Corpse at Duhamel's house on Rue du Château in Paris, a bastion of French Surrealism. This activity fell in line with the Paris vision of Surrealism, since Exquisite Corpse is based on the principles of change and pure psychic automatism advocated by Breton in his first *Surrealist Manifesto* (1924). Although the Brussels Surrealists were somewhat hesitant vis-à-vis automatic writing, they nonetheless dabbled in Exquisite Corpse. René Magritte, Irène Hamoir, Louis Scutenaire, and Marthe and Paul Nougé let their imagination run free to produce perfectly outlandish drawings.

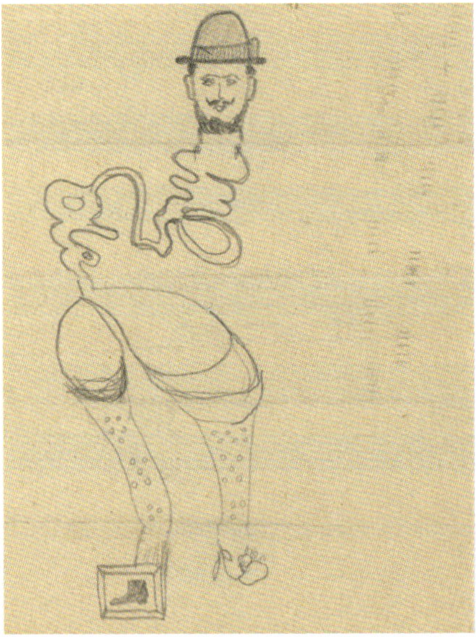

Exquisite Corpse
1934
Pencil on paper
15.4 x 11.8 cm

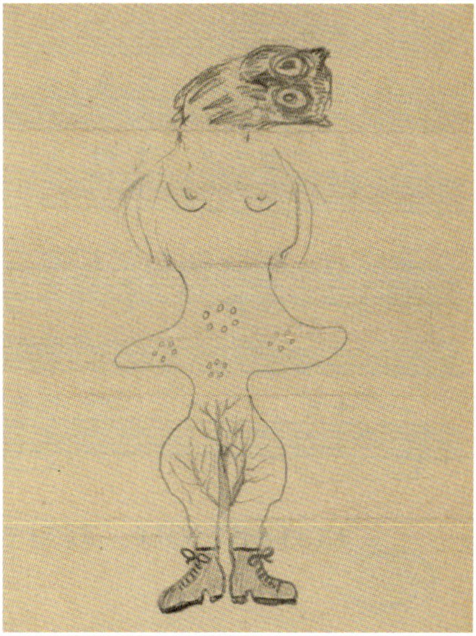

Exquisite Corpse
1934
Pencil on paper
15.4 x 11.9 cm

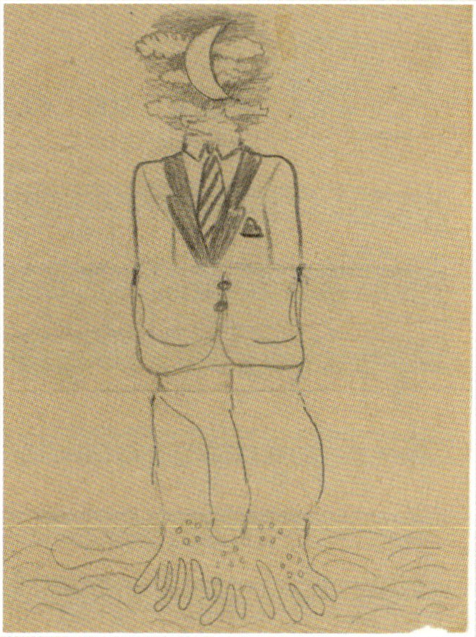

Exquisite Corpse
1934
Pencil on paper
15.4 x 11.9 cm

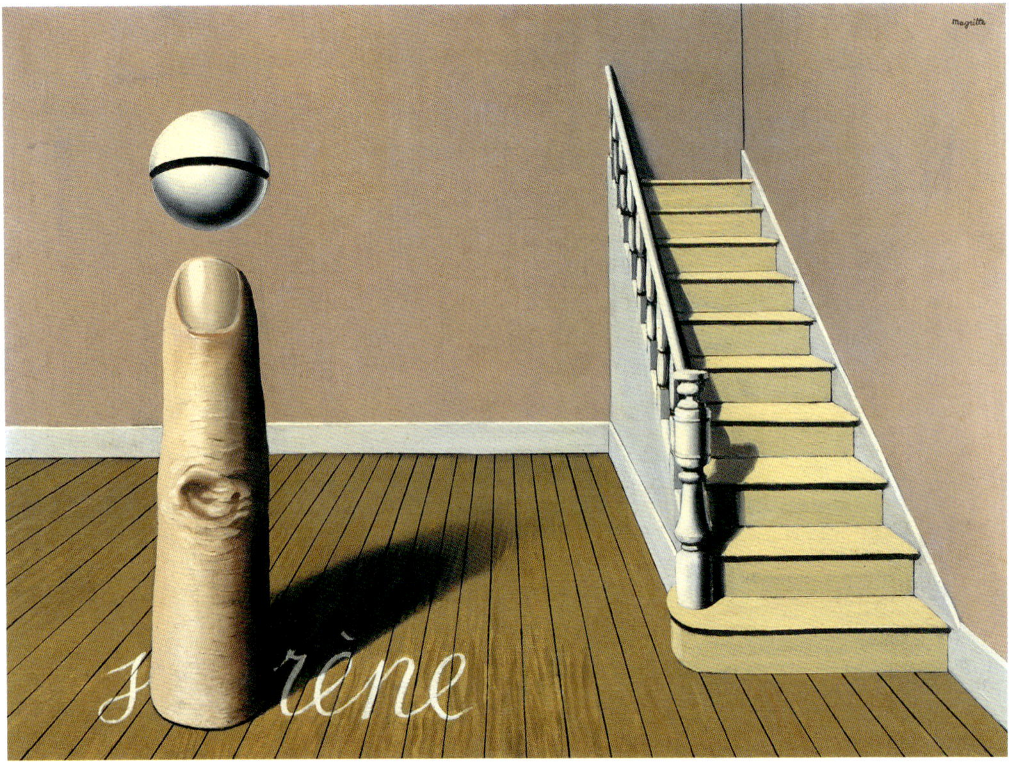

FORBIDDEN LITERATURE

1936
Oil on canvas
54.4 x 73.4 cm
Inv. 11683

Forbidden Literature might be part of an alphabet project that never came to fruition. Constructed around the letter 'i', it reads *sirène*, no doubt in homage to Irène Hamoir, the wife of Louis Scutenaire, Magritte's accomplice in Surrealism. In addition, this upright finger may refer to an erotic novel by Louis Aragon, *Irène's Cunt* (1928) – a theory perhaps confirmed by the staircase that runs into a wall, suggesting the obstacle. Desire and frustration are evoked successively. The sleigh bell dotting the 'i' could corroborate the hypothesis of an erotic allusion. As David Sylvester points out, sleigh bells, which appear frequently in Magritte's work, may have been chosen for their adaptability and perhaps also because of their mysterious form – a slitted sphere – possibly projecting sexual connotations.

GEORGETTE

1937
Oil on canvas
65 x 54 cm
Inv. 10712

In this portrait of Georgette, Magritte reuses several characteristic elements from his pictorial vocabulary: a key, bird, laurel branch, candlestick, glove and scrap of paper with the word 'vague' written on it float around the portrait in a blue sky with white clouds. This strange composition is all the more disturbing in that the sitter seems to be looking at herself in a mirror, a situation that occurs in an earlier *Portrait of Irène Hamoir*. Magritte's repeated use of the mirror shows his interest in it: what we see here is the reflection of Georgette and not Georgette herself, as if the mirror's role is to insist on the difference between a physical person and a painted portrait, between reality and representation. This question lies at the heart of the artist's work. When Magritte was asked about the meaning of this painting, he disavowed all symbolic interpretations. In a letter of June 1957 to his friend Maurice Rapin, he wrote, 'There is no explainable mystery in my painting. The word *Vague* written in the portrait manifests the inexplicable mystery. The objects that accompany my wife's face are no more symbols than the face itself is. My pictures are valid, in my eyes, if the objects they represent resist interpretation as symbols and other explanations.'

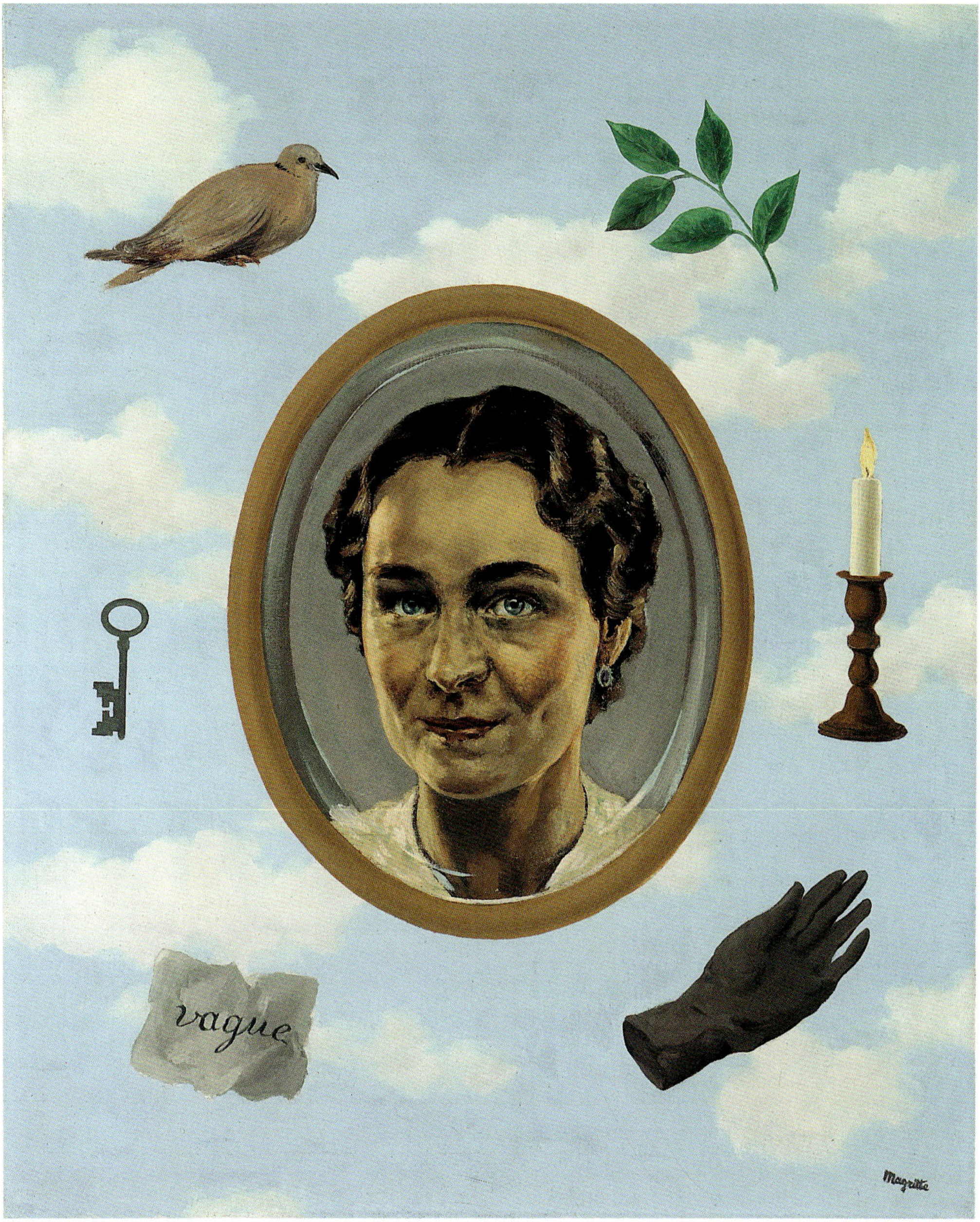
vague
Magritte

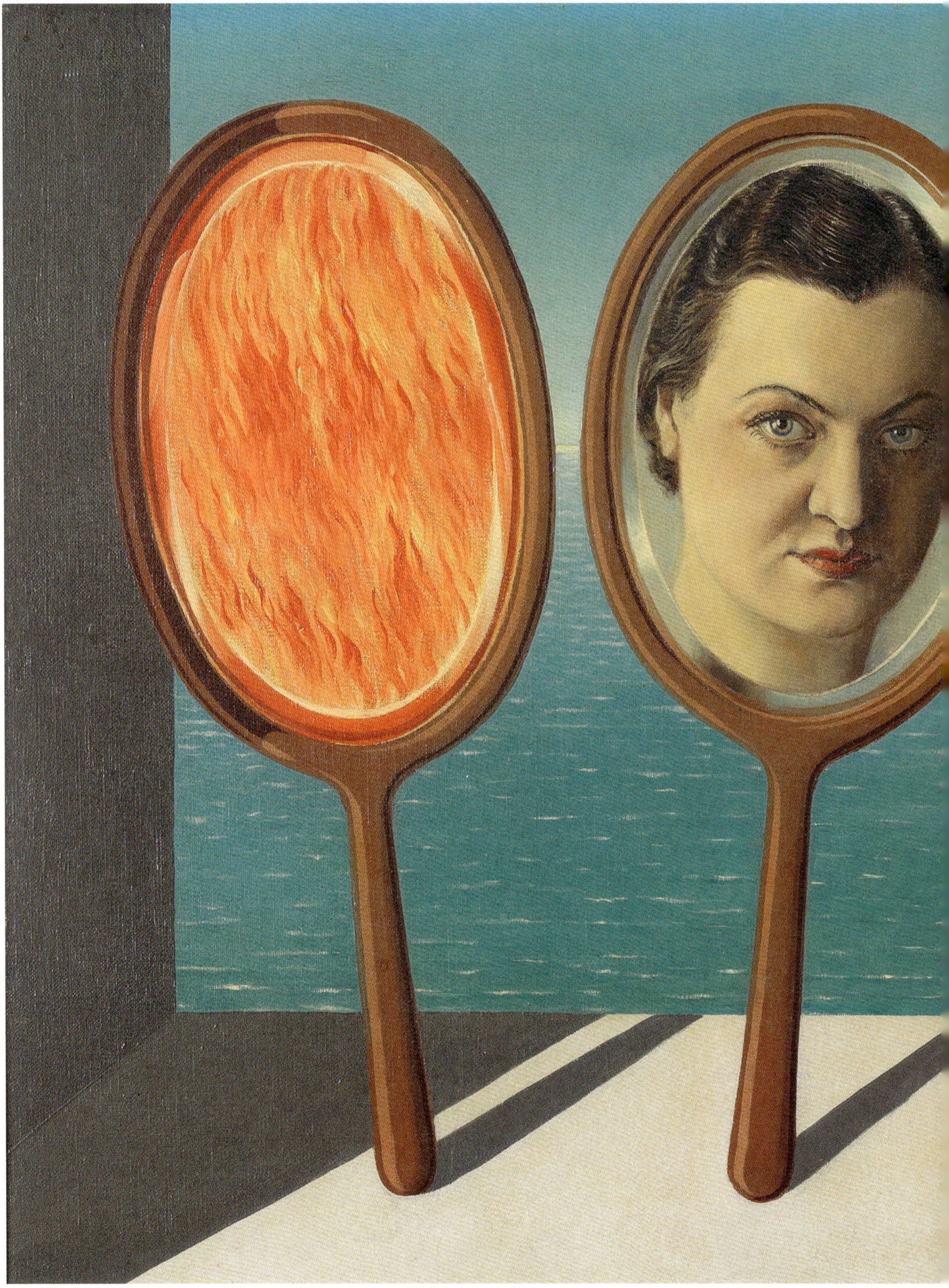

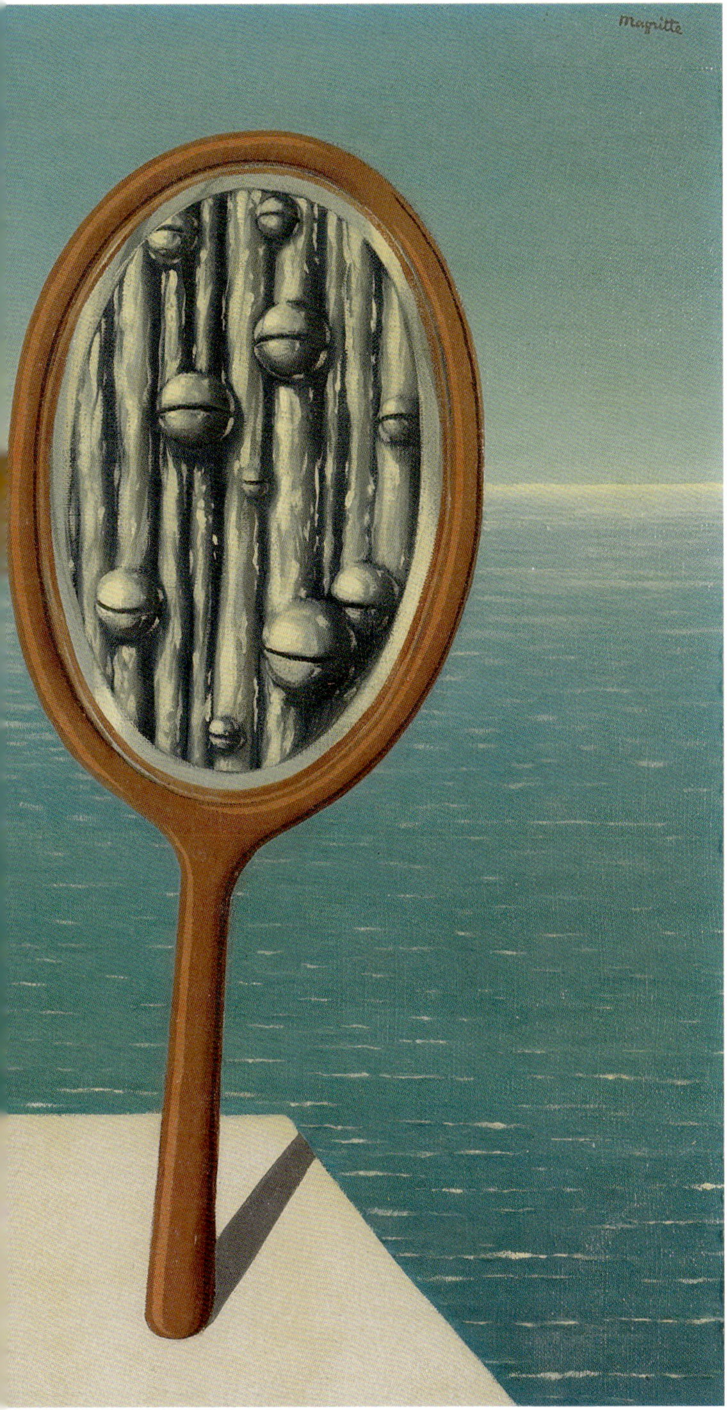

Portrait of Irène Hamoir

1936
Oil on canvas
54.5 x 73.5 cm
Inv. 11682

PHOTOGRAPHY

Magritte's approach to photography in the 1930s parallels his approach to cinema twenty years later. Like his films, his photographs made no claim to art. They essentially meant to record for posterity good times spent among friends. Magritte did not explore the medium's creative potential, which developed considerably between the wars through movements like Subjective Photography. With Louis Scutenaire, Paul Nougé, E. L. T. Mesens and many others, Magritte always proceeded in the same manner, working out a setting and composing a scene in detail, arranging the figures and objects as he would for a painting. The resulting figures in unexpected surroundings and poses echo the painter's pictorial world, sense of humour and predilection for the out-of-the-ordinary as a source of mystery and unsettling strangeness. The creative and poetic approach of Magritte, who 'set up' his photographs, no doubt counterbalances the objectivity the medium was criticized for, an objectivity whereby the 'relationships in which the object presents itself to the lens are recorded without flights of fancy'. Magritte used photography in a traditional manner, in its most usual sense of recording reality, but a previously modified, thought-out and invented reality. *The Fidelity of the Images*, a portfolio published posthumously in 1976, comprises sixteen photographs with titles given by Louis Scutenaire. Though an exception, it is worth drawing attention to because some of the photographs were the inspiration for paintings. *God, the Eighth Day* (1937), for example, gave rise to the iconography of *The Healer*.

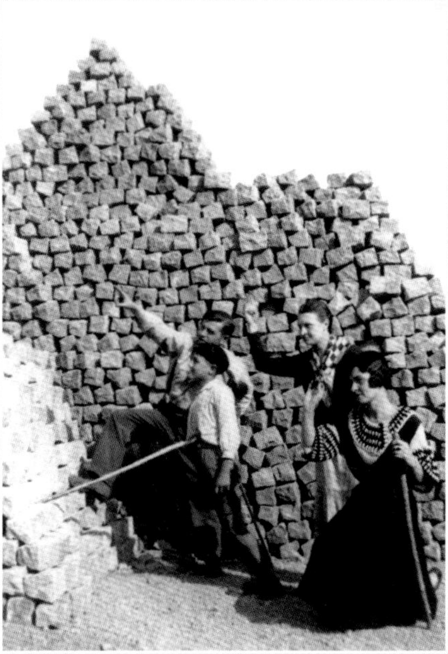

The Fidelity of the Images: The Pharaohs of the Eighth Dynasty, Lessines, August 1935

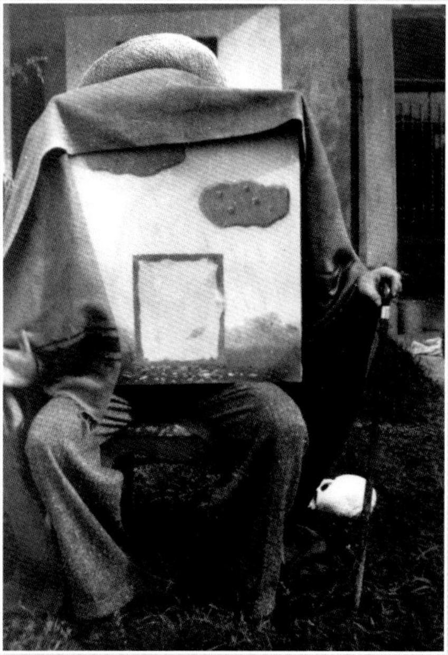

The Fidelity of the Images: God, the Eighth Day, Jette (Brussels), 1937

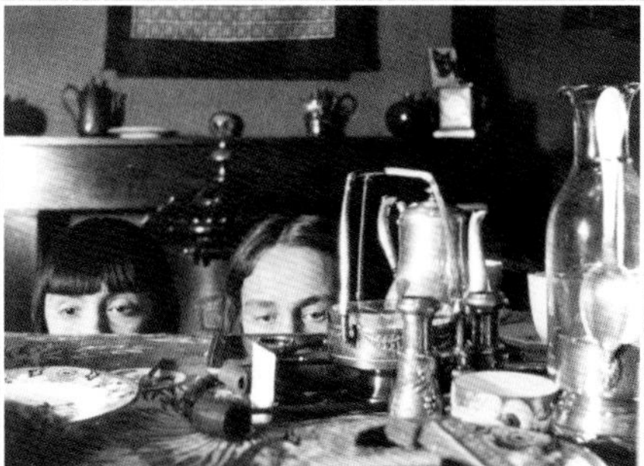

The Fidelity of the Images: The Clairvoyants, Brussels, 1930

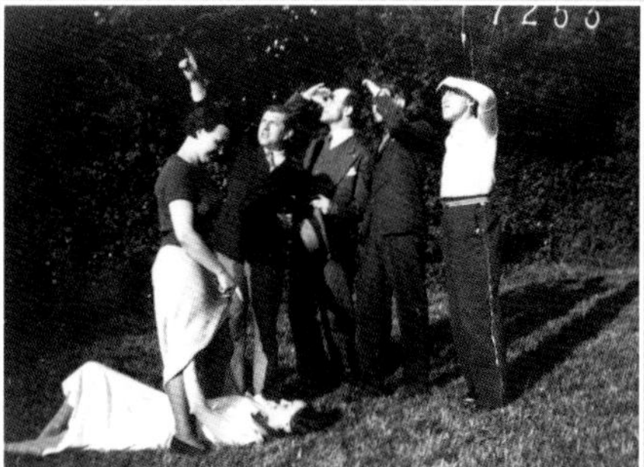

The Fidelity of the Images: The Eclipse, Beersel, July 1935

BEL CANTO

1938
Oil on canvas
73.5 x 54.7 cm
Inv. 11684

A dream that Magritte told to Edward James in 1939 could be the source of this painting: 'I was visited one night by an ambassador of the country where living rooms are lit with candles, he was a curious personage composed of irregular marble plaques of night on which the words "Bel Canto" were engraved in calligraphy. He was a tall man and hid a large part of a winter landscape, with a very luminous blue sky above snow-covered roofs.' While Magritte seems to be revealing the origin of this image, Louis Scutenaire, who bought the painting just after it was finished, gives another version of the story: 'He went out to buy milk one winter morning, and between him and the snow-covered houses there suddenly loomed a huge building with blackish forms – dark slabs attached to each other or one atop the other bearing the inscription "Bel Canto". He made a faithful painting of this vision and called it "Bel Canto".'

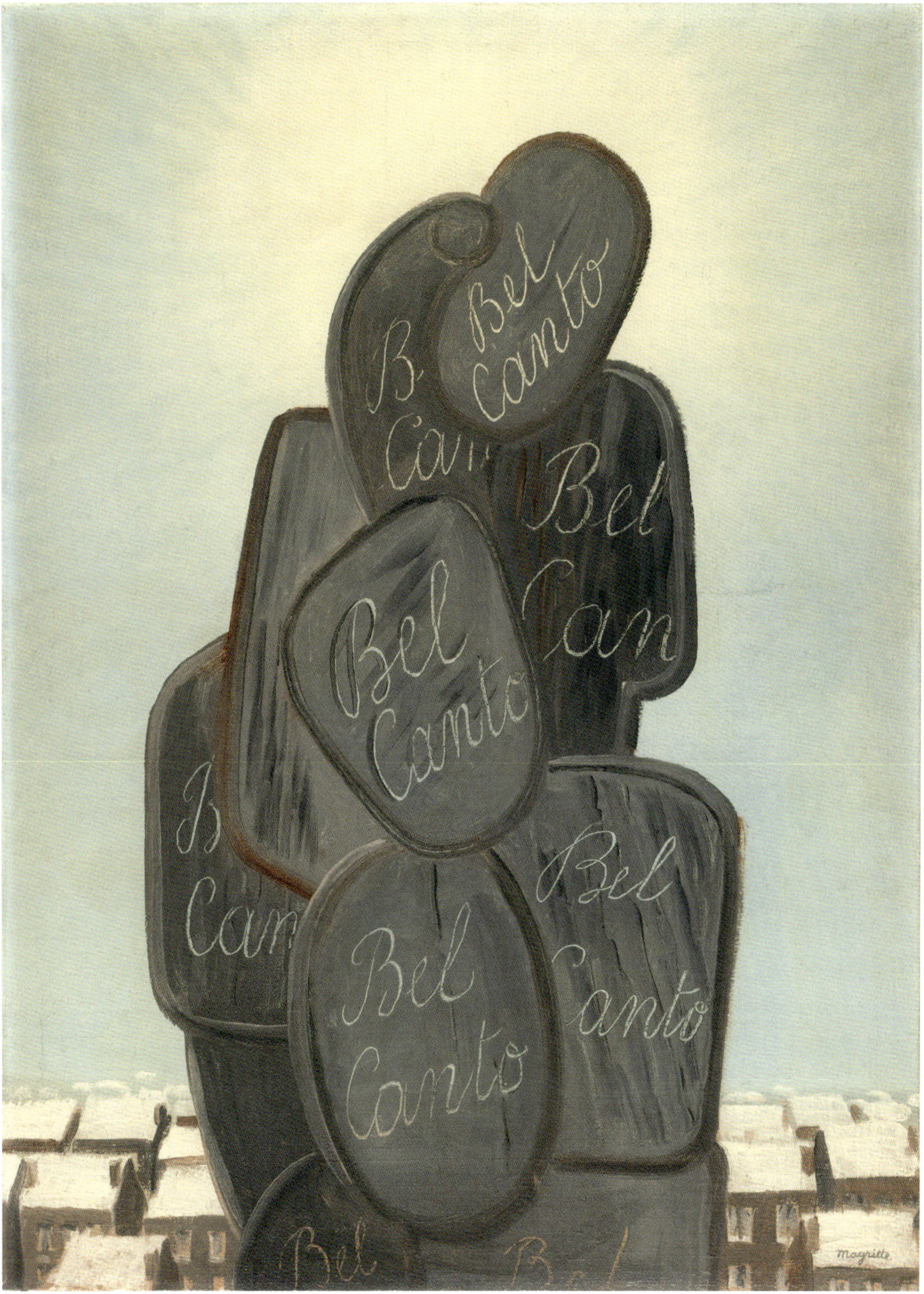
Bel Canto
B Can
Bel Can
Bel Canto
B Can
Bel Canto
Bel anto
Bel
Bel
magritte

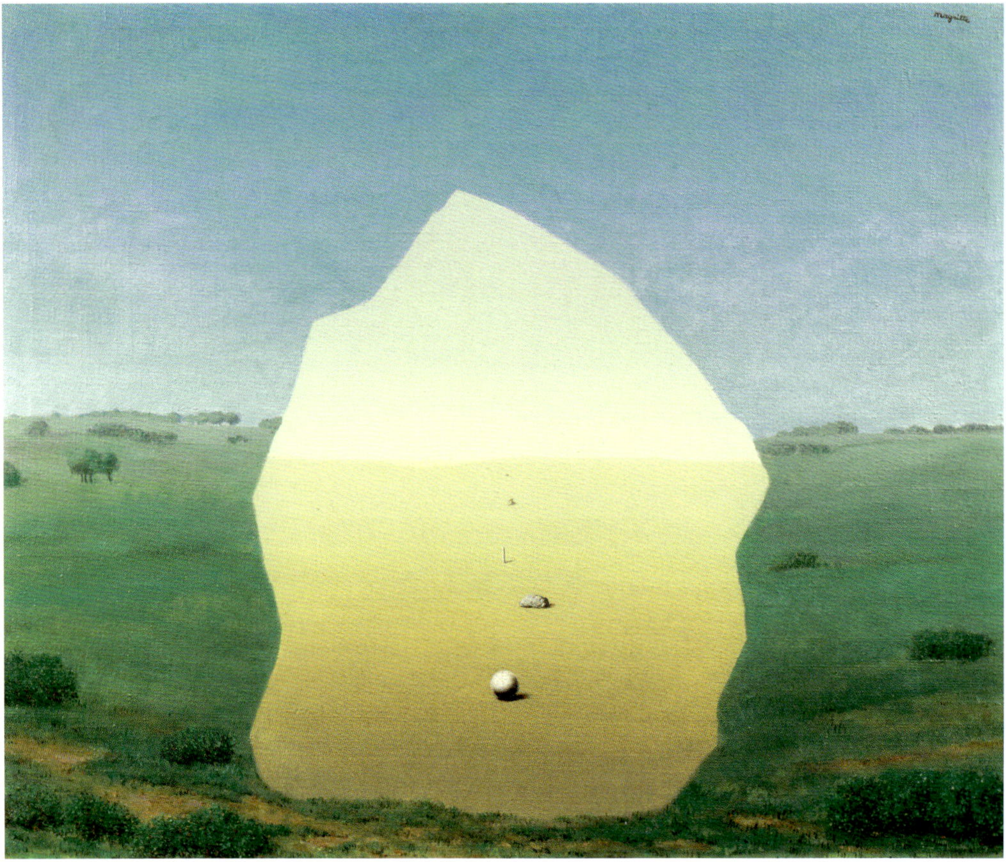

The Kiss

1938
Oil on canvas
60 x 74 cm
Inv. 10229

Magritte wrote to Paul Eluard that he had done a painting called *The Kiss*: 'It is a country landscape completely devoid of interest. It covers the entire surface of the painting, except that in the centre, an opening in the land and sky looks out onto a distance beyond the landscape surrounding it. This vista is strewn with objects, first a rock, then a sphere, then some twisted wire, then a stick standing in the ground; past that, nothing can be made out clearly.' This opening onto a desert landscape and the dizzying perspective created by the objects littering the ground recall the infinite horizons painted by other Surrealists, like Salvador Dalí and Yves Tanguy. However, the source of this work may have been a photograph. When visiting Roland Penrose in April 1938, Magritte could have seen the American photographer Lee Miller's *Portrait of Space* hanging on the wall. It depicts a screen with a hole in it that opens onto the Siwa Desert.

THE RETURN

1940
Oil on canvas
50.2 x 65 cm
Inv. 6667

In a letter to the writer Claude Spaak dated November 1940, Magritte refers to his painting projects and mentions a 'blue bird with clouds in front of a starry sky; in the foreground, a nest with eggs'. A bird and its nest appeared in 1938 with the first version of *The Domain of Arnheim*. In that work, however, the bird is frozen and transformed into a mountain of stone, in contrast to the freedom of flight conveyed here. When Magritte painted this canvas, he was back in Brussels after spending time in the south of France. He had taken refuge there at the beginning of the Nazi occupation of Belgium, leaving Georgette to stay with her sister. The couple's reunion after three months' separation was a joyful one. This work could be a double response to not only Magritte's return to his wife but also the war: a diurnal bird, symbol of freedom, soars through the darkness of night. Besides the interplay of day and night, which is also central to the many variants of *The Dominion of Light*, the motif of the bird reappears in other paintings, including *Sky Bird* (1966), which was the emblem of the former Belgian airline Sabena.

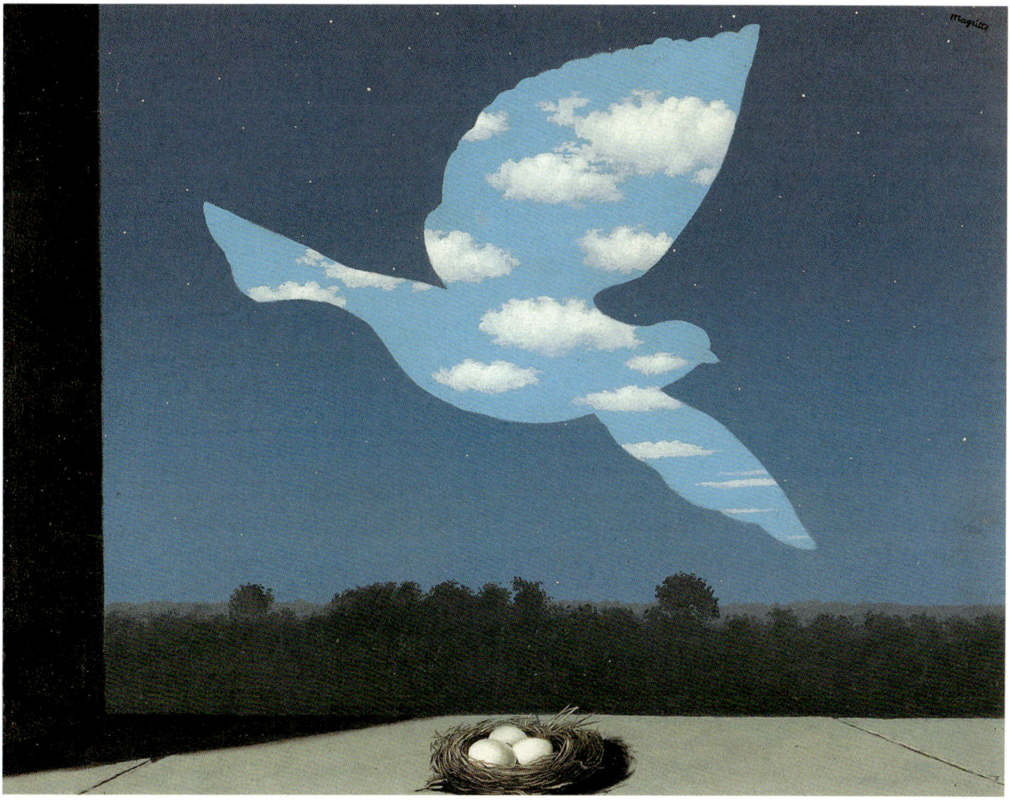
magritte

The Companions of Fear

1942
Gouache on paper
33 x 48.5 cm
Inv. 11678

The title, chosen by Louis Scutenaire, is from the detective novel *The League of Frightened Men*, written in 1935 by the American Rex Stout, whose stories Magritte enjoyed. (The novel was published in French translation as *Les Compagnons de la peur.*) The figure of a plant gradually metamorphosing into a bird appeared in 1942 in two guises: a dove (*Treasure Island*) and an owl (*The Companions of Fear*). If the underlying concept is identical, the sensation felt in looking at these two works and the atmosphere that emanates from them are quite different, owing to the palette and the choice of title and literary reference. Painted under the Nazi occupation, these two works are like pendants corresponding to two human feelings inextricably linked to wartime: the fear of death and the hope of freedom. *The Companions of Fear* reflects the former, a feeling of anguish suggested by the presence of these inauspicious nocturnal birds with their fixed gaze. In contrast, *Treasure Island* (the title is from the book by Robert Louis Stevenson) inspires a feeling of hope, although the doves' wings are spread under a grey sky, and the birds are on the ground as if unable to fly. The historical context of Magritte's works should be taken into consideration, especially between 1940 and 1945. Here, we are on the threshold of a strong reaction to the war on the part of the artist, who was about to produce the first works of his 'Sunlit' period, declaring 'We mustn't fear sunlight just because it almost always serves to illuminate a miserable world.'

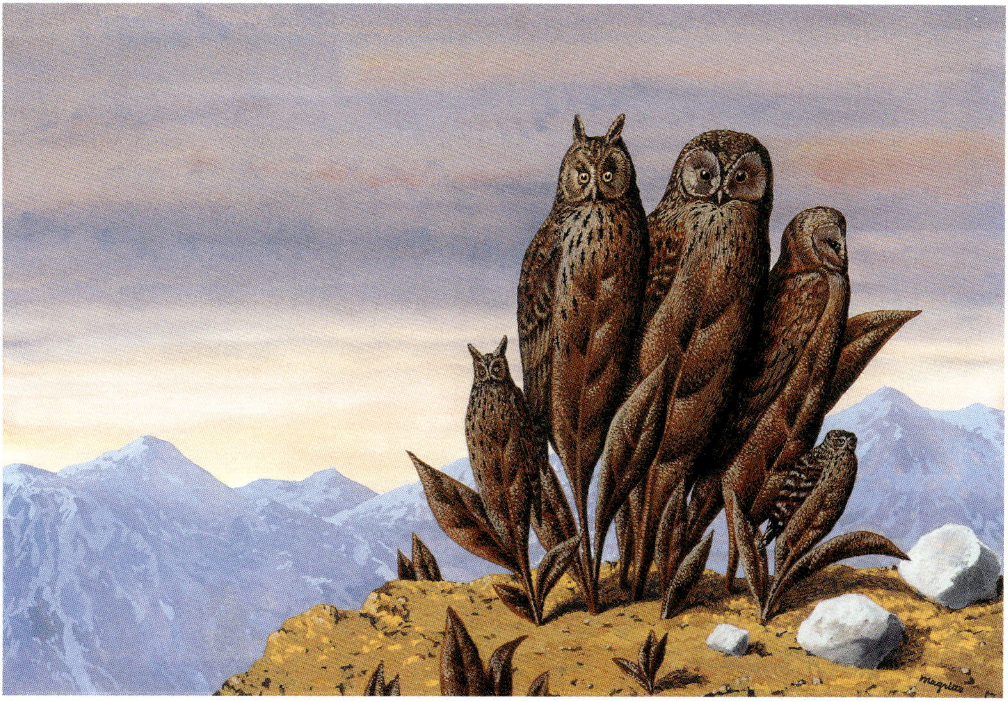

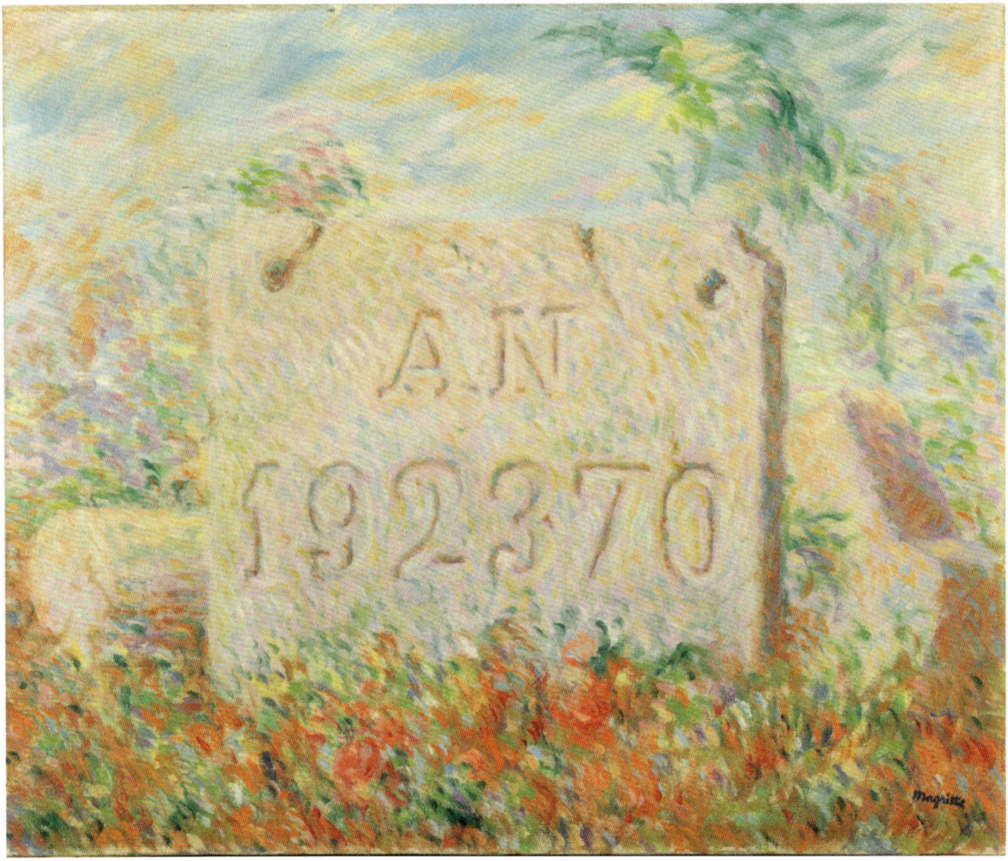
AN
192370
Magritte

THE SMILE

1943
Oil on canvas
54 x 65 cm
Inv. 11686

The Smile is from Magritte's 'Sunlit' period, which lasted from 1943 to 1948. This period, also called 'Surrealism in Full Sunlight' and the 'Renoir' period, is characterized by an Impressionist-style brushstroke and a new, much brighter, more luminous range of colours. 'Since the start of the war . . . I have keenly wanted a new poetic effectiveness that would provide charm and pleasure. I leave it to others to upset, terrorize and persist in confusing everything.' Standing up for hope and joy at the height of World War II, the artist painted nearly seventy canvases and fifty gouaches in this style. However, 'Surrealism in Full Sunlight' did not appeal to anyone, and the artist was forced to return to his previous style.

The Blaze

1943
Oil on canvas
54 x 65 cm
Inv. 10710

This canvas was entitled *The Blaze* by Louis Scutenaire. The agitated brushstroke and warm, reddish colouration make it a new emblem of 'Surrealism in Full Sunlight'. The iconography reuses a formula that appeared in 1935 with *The Giantess*. While pursuing the problematological investigation begun ten years earlier with *Elective Affinities*, *The Unexpected Answer* and *The Human Condition*, Magritte wrote to Breton in July 1934, 'At the moment, I am trying to find in a tree what belongs to it well and proper but would nevertheless deny our notion of a tree.' And he found the solution: 'The tree, as a problem object, became a large leaf whose stem was a trunk rooted directly into the ground. I named it "The Giantess", after a poem by Baudelaire.' In *The Blaze*, this leaf-tree multiplies into a forest of giant leaves that reach the sky and at the same time play on proportions and scale, a device Magritte was fond of and used many times from the mid-1930s on.

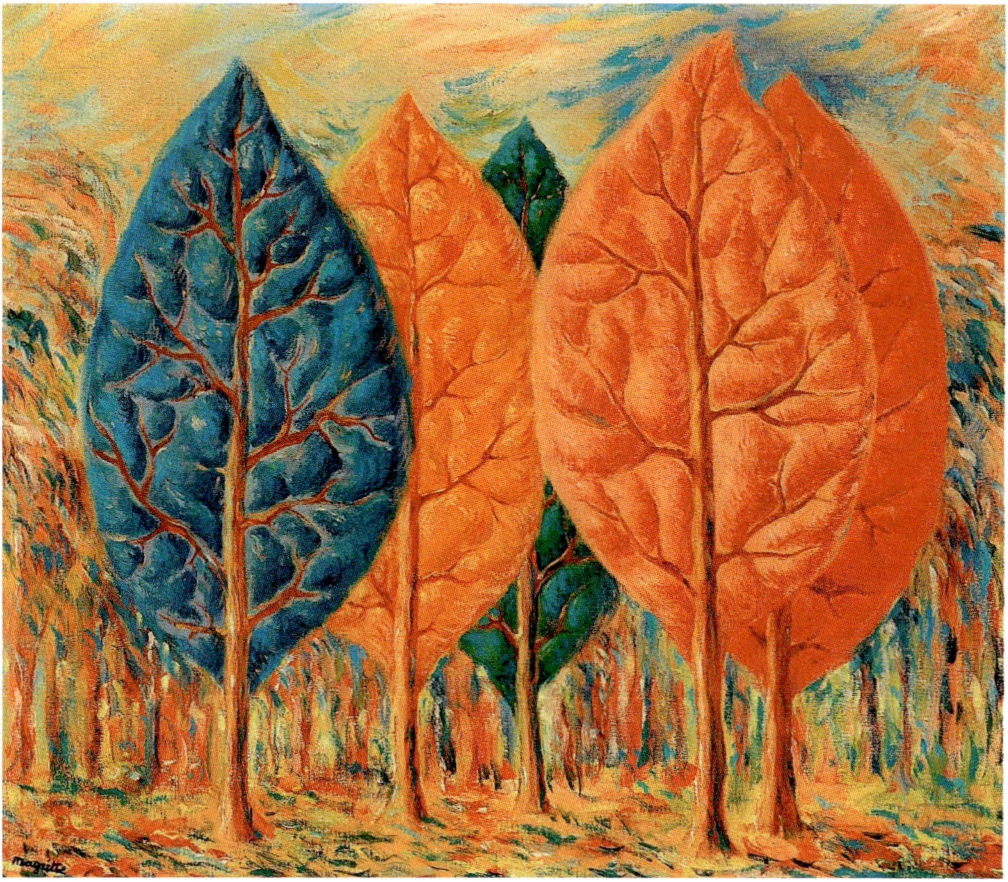
Magritte

Natural Encounters

1945
Oil on canvas
81 x 65.3 cm
Inv. 11690

In *Natural Encounters*, Magritte brings two bilboquets to life. They are wearing antique-style red drapes and looking in different directions. One brandishes a leaf as a gift from the heavens that appear through two windows irrationally and asymmetrically outlined in the pinkish wall. Magritte commented on this work in the booklet *Dix tableaux de Magritte* [Ten Paintings by Magritte]: 'Two wooden figures are in a room. In the wall, a tilted window.' This purely objective description of what viewers can see for themselves is of no help in understanding the work. Nor is the title, which is only meant to befuddle. The figure of the bilboquet with a head extended by a cannon-shaped snout recurred many times and coincides with the process – already observed with the bowling pin – of endowing inanimate objects with life. In *Roses of Picardy*, from 1925, a bowling pin is given a wide-open eye. The Surrealists were fascinated by the eye, and it became a central theme in the art of Magritte and his contemporaries. The painter, who devoted an entire painting to the representation of an eye (*The False Mirror*), points out that 'the art of painting is an art of thinking. Its existence emphasizes the importance of the role played by the human eye in life; indeed the only sense with which a picture is concerned is that of sight.' One of the most influential scenes in the history of Surrealist film is centred on the visual capacity: in the first minutes of *Un chien andalou* (1929), an eye shown in close-up is slit with a razor-blade.

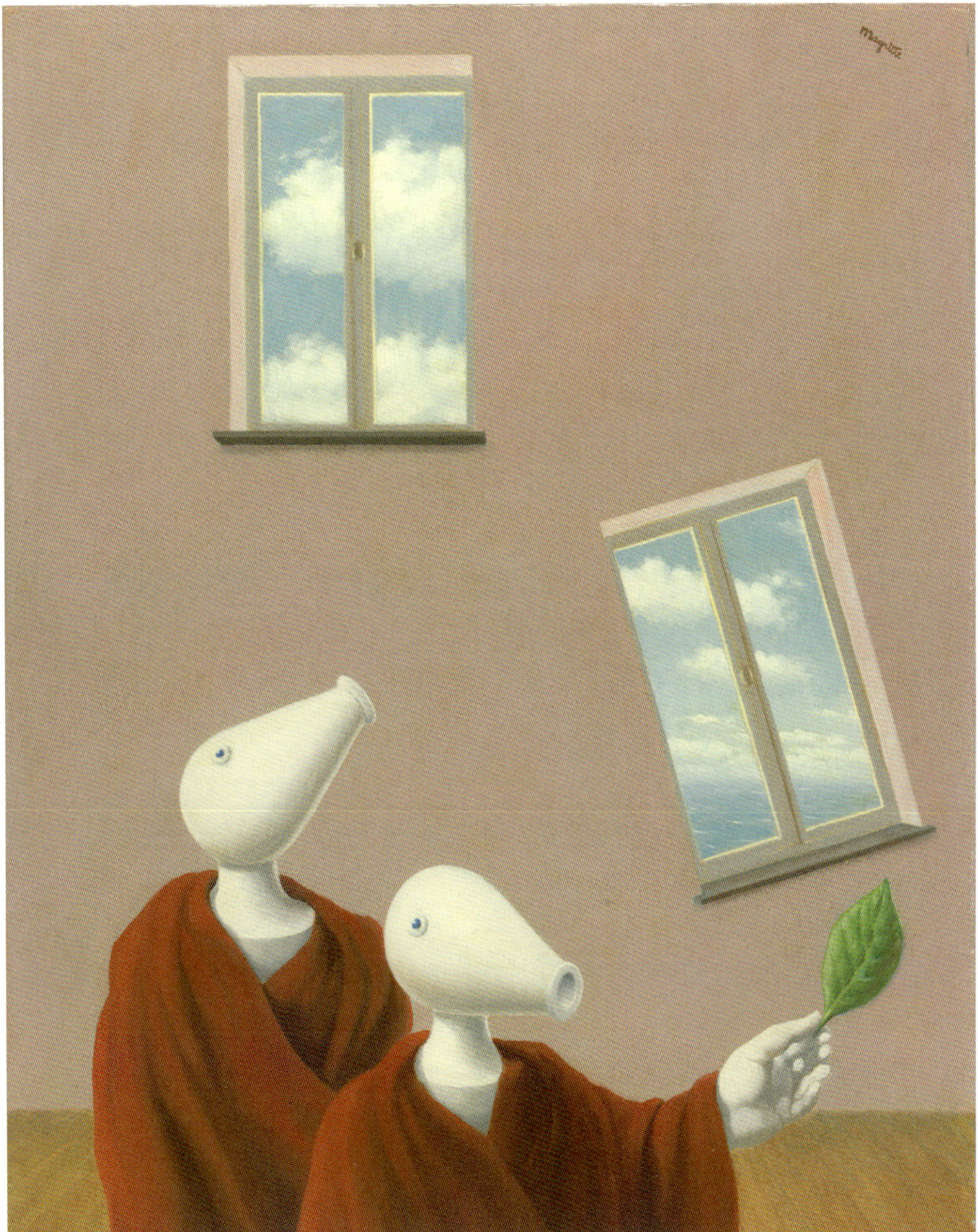
Magritte

Black Magic

1945
Oil on canvas
79 x 59 cm
Inv. 10706

'All I know about the hope I place in love is that only a woman can give it reality.' Magritte, in love with women since his early youth, never stopped depicting the eternal feminine in different forms and poses. By transforming the sky into the flesh of Georgette, his wife and favourite model, Magritte admitted to committing 'an act of black magic'. The theme of the metamorphosis of flesh into blue sky, which first appeared in 1934, always involves the portrayal of a standing nude woman, frontal or in profile, whose body gradually turns colour and subtly blends into the aerial background. According to Magritte in a letter of 1934 to André Breton, it is this two-tone body 'that immediately seduced art lovers with its pretty colours'. Taking into account the taste of art lovers is a feature of the painter's work, although he often denied that he made commercial art. When Magritte found an effective idea that could lead to a *successful* image, that is an image that could resist all explanation, he produced it in various forms. Details may change, but the initial concept remains. For this reason, variants of the same work are frequent with Magritte.

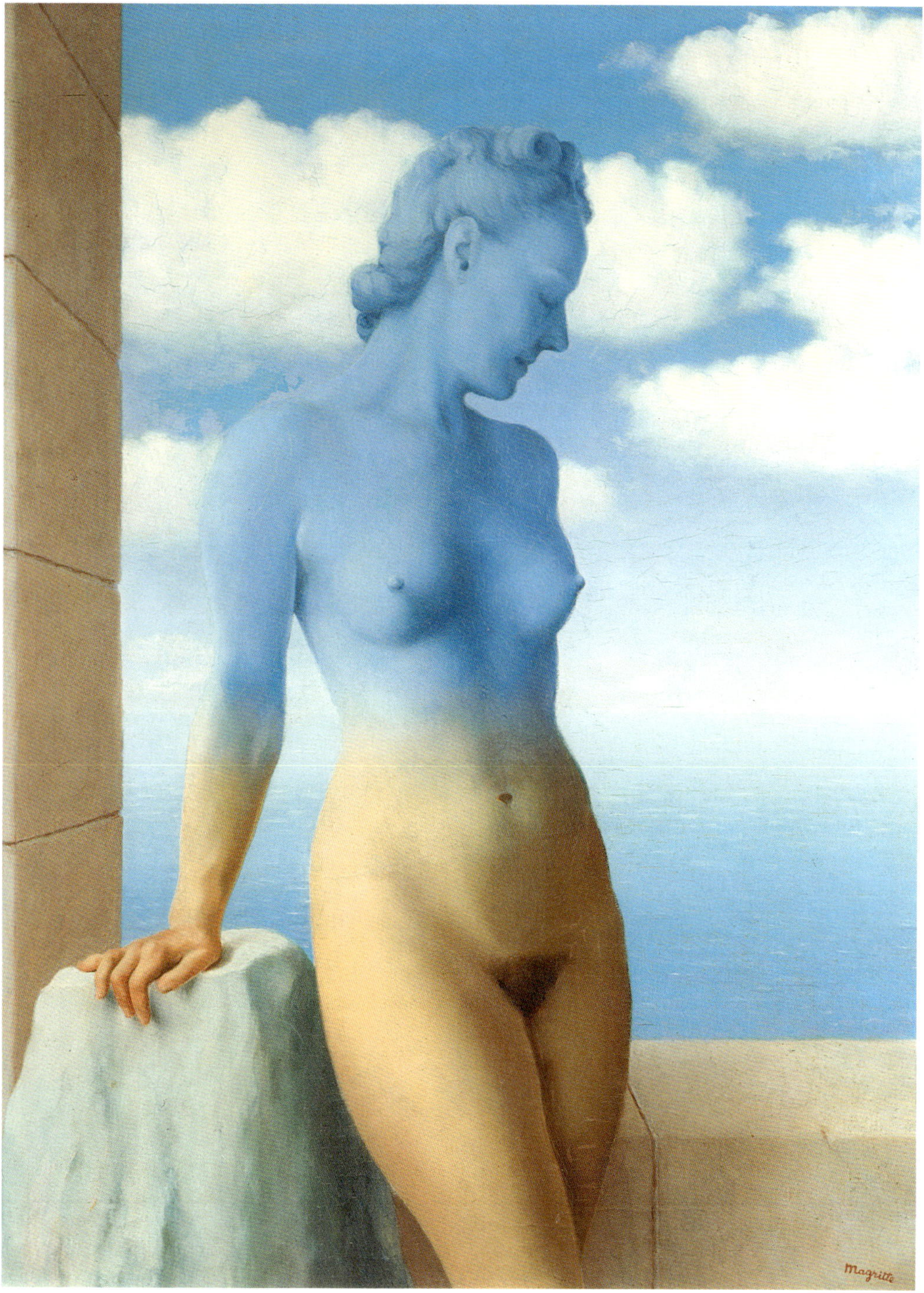
Magritte

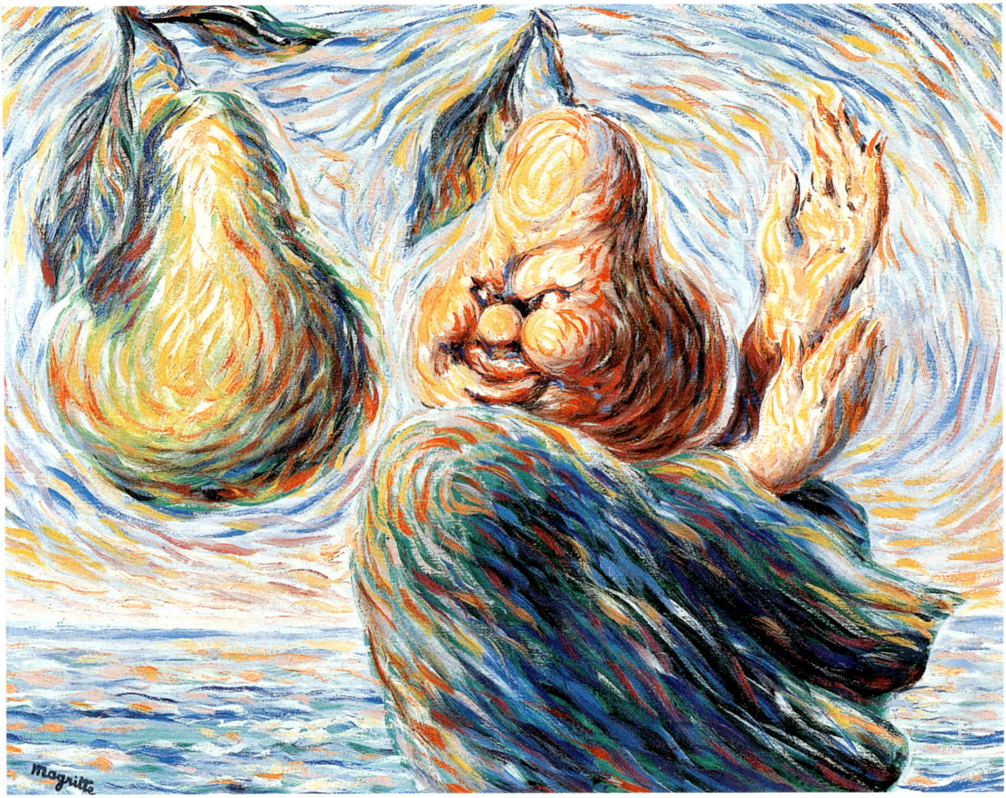
Magritte

Lyricism

1947
Oil on canvas
50.5 x 65 cm
Inv. 11693

This transitional canvas employs the luminous palette and lively brushstroke of the 'Sunlit' period, while the nervous, almost crude character of the gesture (much closer to Van Gogh than to Renoir) and the overall satirical atmosphere herald the 'Vache' period (1948). In this image, Magritte is referring to a 19th-century French artist. The idea of converting a head into a pear originated with Honoré Daumier, whose famous caricature of King Louis-Philippe, *Les Poires* (1831), transforms the sovereign's head in four steps. Magritte was interested in caricature and returned to it a year later in a series of works openly aimed at making fun of the French Surrealists, known as Magritte's 'Vache' period.

The Ellipsis

1948
Oil on canvas
50.3 x 73 cm
Inv. 11695

The Ellipsis is from a series of paintings Magritte made in March and April 1948. Grouped together under the heading of the 'Vache' period, they are the consequence of Magritte's experience in Paris and the failures he met with, first in 1924, then in 1930. In 1947, he was brusquely excommunicated from the Surrealist movement by André Breton, who, referring to 'Surrealism in Full Sunlight', compared him to 'a backward child who to ensure himself a pleasant day would immobilize the barometer's needle at "permanent sunshine"'. Magritte then decided to thumb his nose at the Paris public and the French Surrealists. With the avowed goal of 'really making an impression on them', he painted seventeen canvases and a dozen gouaches in a very crude style, a thousand light-years from the smooth brushwork and detailed rendering of his early years. Exhibited at the Galerie du Faubourg, Paris, in 1948, these works were poorly received by Breton and company, who failed to grasp the profoundly Surrealist act Magritte had committed.

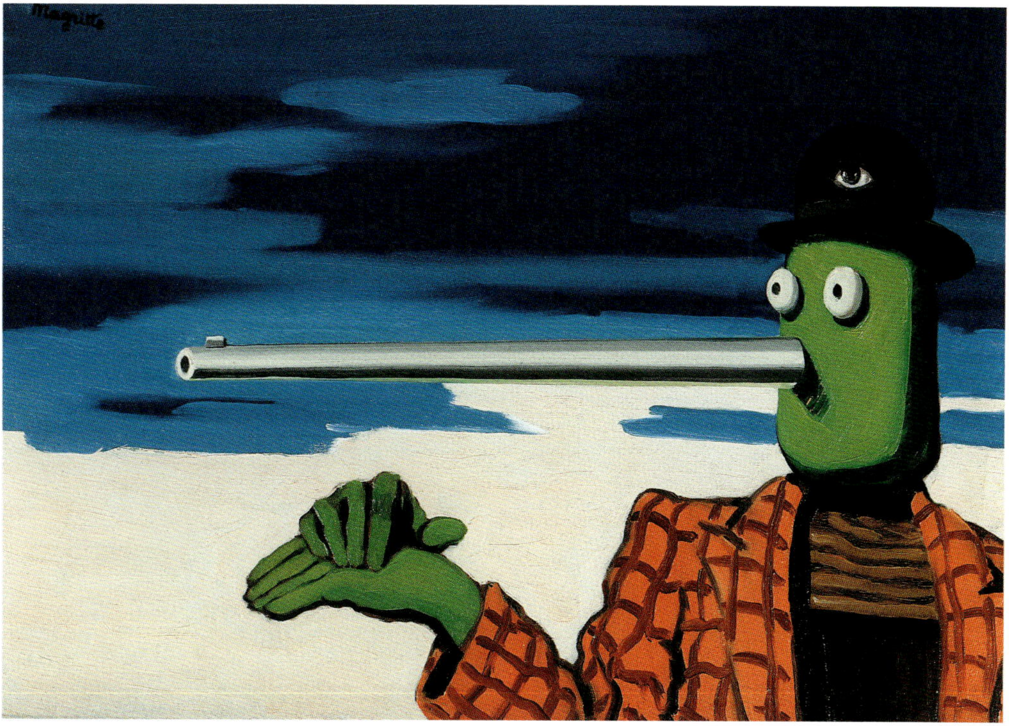
Magritte

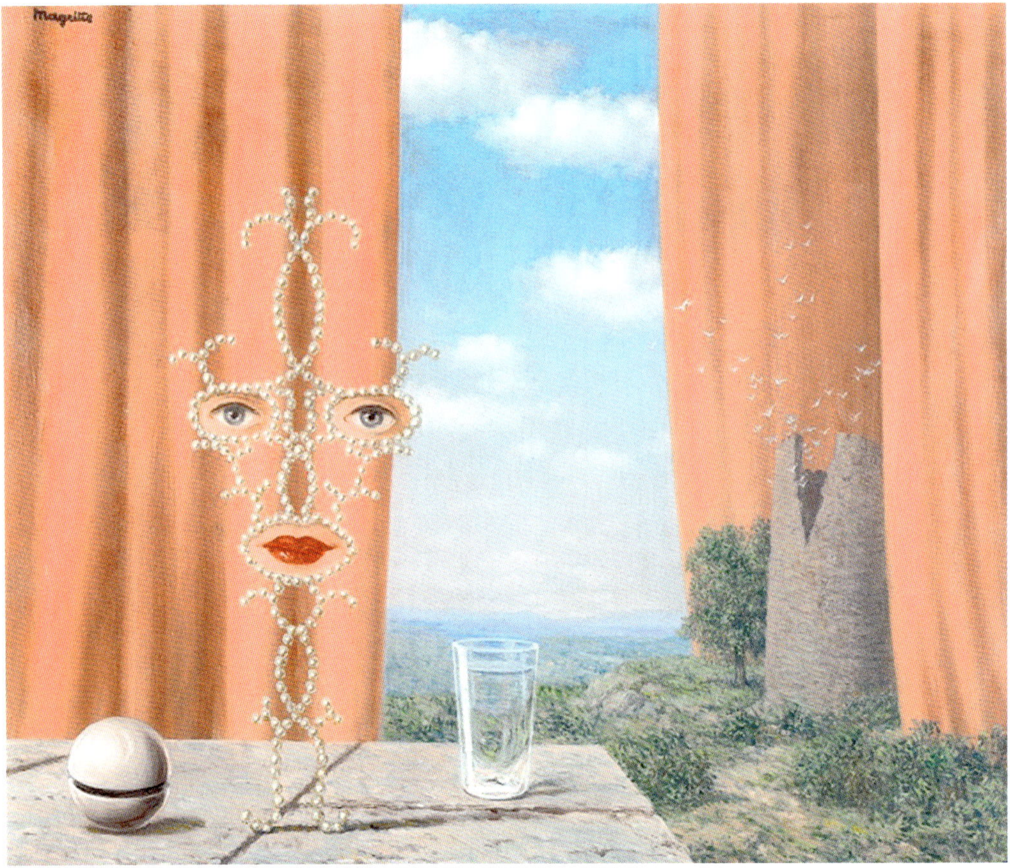
Magritte

Scheherazade

1948
Oil on canvas
50 x 60 cm
Inv. 11566

Magritte read *The Thousand and One Nights* during the summer of 1946, which accounts for the choice of *Scheherazade* as the title for this pearl-woman object. It is one of the most widespread themes in Magritte's œuvre. All told, there are no fewer than twenty oil and gouache variants on this motif. An exhibition at the Lou Cosyn gallery in Brussels in 1947 offered visitors a variety of versions of the theme. Conceived during the period of 'Surrealism in Full Sunlight', this seductive iconography that emphasizes the 'beautiful side of life' was treated in different styles – the Impressionist style of the period, but also the more realistic style seen here that nonetheless retains a memory of the lighter, brighter palette of the 'Sunlit' period. This work once again combines such recurrent elements from Magritte's vocabulary as the sleigh bell, blue sky with clouds, theatre curtains and a glass of water, which is most often set on a balustrade. Magritte said of this work, 'The series where one sees eyes and mouths encrusted with pearls enriches our spirit with a new concept which makes the boundaries of reason recede.'

THE FLAVOUR OF TEARS

1948
Oil on canvas
60 x 50 cm
Inv. 6804

While *Black Magic* and *Scheherazade* attest to Magritte's practice of producing variants, this work is the result of a different procedure – exact replication. It is the only known case in the painter's œuvre of two completely identical canvases, the other one being at the Barber Institute of Fine Arts in Birmingham, England. They have the same dimensions, date, signature in the lower left, and mention of title and date on the back. Much has been written about this exception. Marcel Mariën offers a plausible explanation in 'Le Jumeau d'Amérique [The American Twin]', an essay published in 1984. He believes that Magritte reproduced the work identically to satisfy two clients interested in buying the same painting. This canvas furthermore announces Magritte's return to his previous style. The leaf-bird had appeared in *Treasure Island* in 1942, except that there, it is not eaten by a caterpillar. This sad image with its leaden atmosphere marks a radical break with 'Surrealism in Full Sunlight'. It is perhaps symptomatic of a post-war era that was difficult both for humanity, which had to rebuild itself, and for Magritte, who received little support from his contemporaries. After 1948, he was compelled to abandon 'Surrealism in Full Sunlight' and the 'Vache' period because of the harsh criticism they drew. At this time, he met Alexander Iolas, who became his official dealer in the United States and thanks to whom he developed an American clientele. Iolas strongly advised him to return to the style he had evolved in the 1940s and produce variants for the American market. This relationship signalled the beginning of René Magritte's international success.

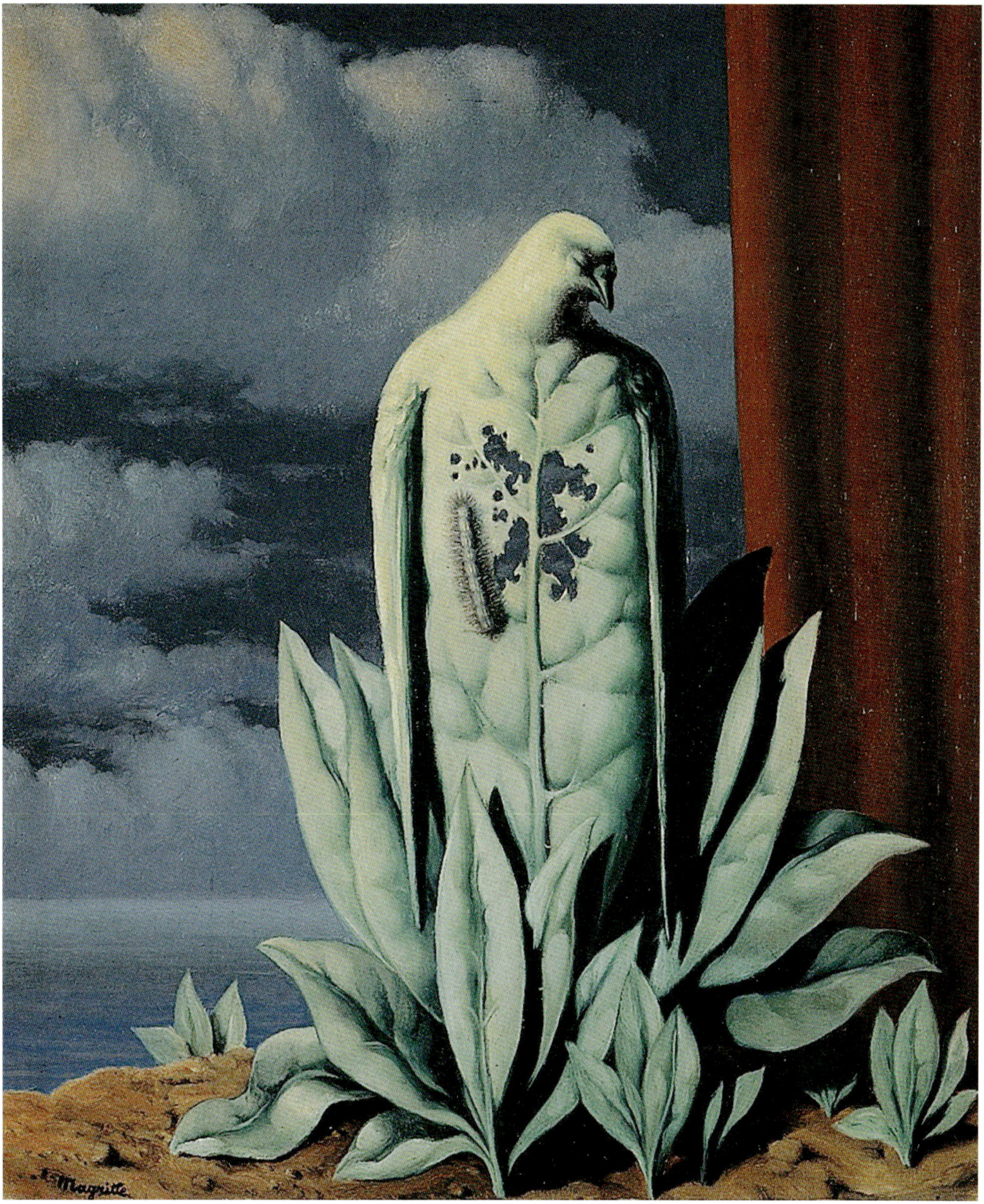
Magritte

THE DOMINION OF LIGHT

1954
Oil on canvas
146 x 114 cm
Inv. 6715

The Dominion of Light is perhaps the most emblematic of all René Magritte's paintings. Produced in many variants between 1949 and 1965, this major work parallels other paintings, like *Great Expectations* (1940), in that the components of the composition are all based on reality. There are no bewildering combinations of objects, metamorphoses or tampering with proportions. Rather, our mental habits are disturbed by an overpoweringly mysterious reality. At first, it is difficult to detect exactly what it is that 'doesn't add up', so pervasive is the composition's cohesion. The luminous daytime sky over this nocturnal scene offers a solution to the problem of how to represent day and night simultaneously, just as *In Praise of the Dialectic* solves the problem of how to represent inside and outside at the same time. Pursuing his problematological approach here, Magritte offers an image that is all the more powerful for seeming real. The care lavished on the rendering of the details, the reflections on the surface of the water and the glow of the street lamp, as well as the open invitation to the imagination before these lit windows where anything might take place, are the means of enabling the impossible and causing a poetic shock that leaves viewers in confusion. 'This evocation of night and day seems to me to possess the power to surprise and enchant us. I call this power "poetry". If I think that this evocation has such poetic power, it is because, among other things, I have always had the greatest interest in night and day, yet without ever feeling a preference for one over the other.' Commissioned in 1954 by the Royal Museums of Fine Arts of Belgium, this vertical version, of which there are three similar variants, is one of the most imposing.

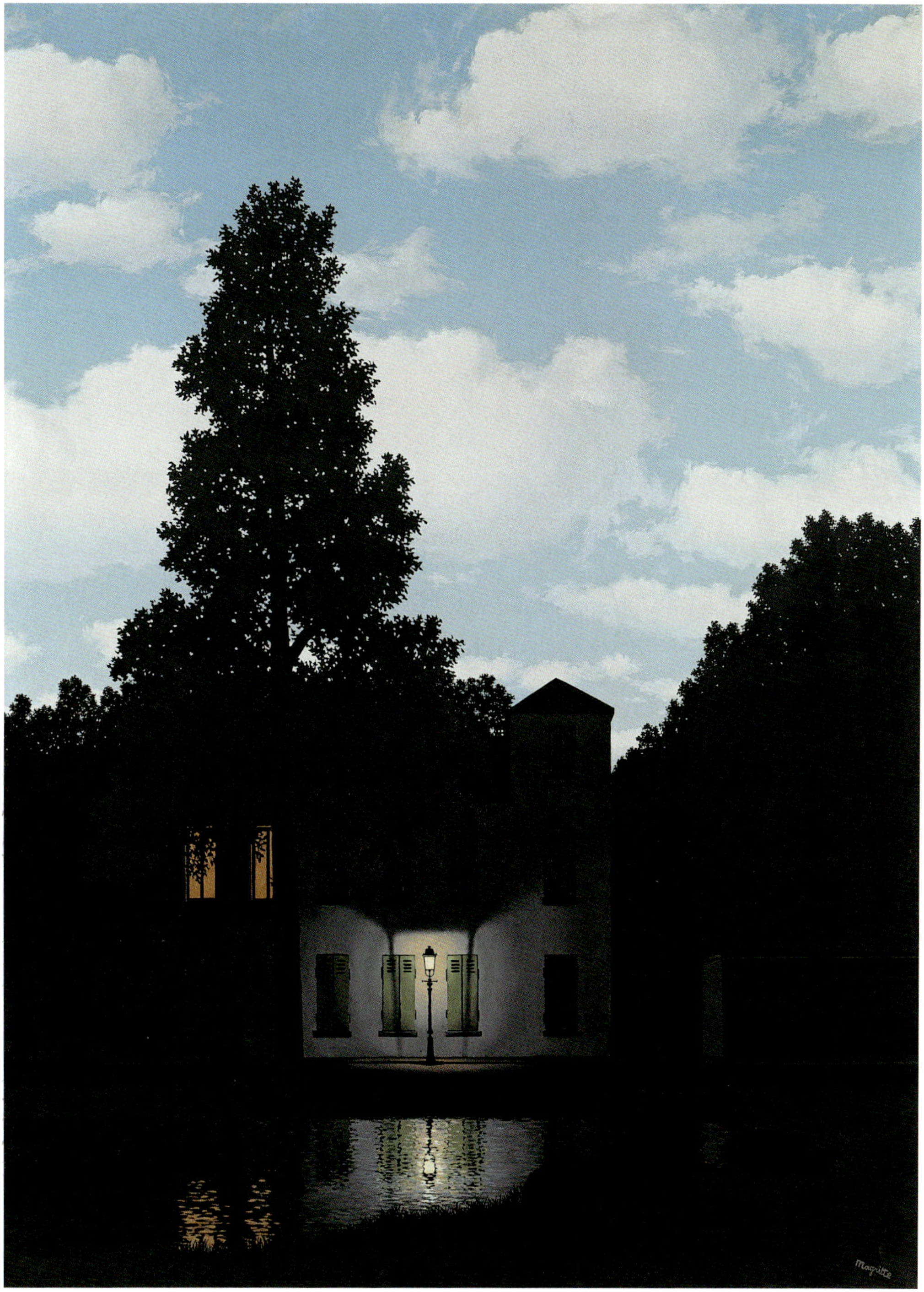
Magritte

FILMS

Cinema takes various forms in the work of René Magritte. However, it should be made clear that the movies he liked were popular slapstick comedies. His collection of silent movies, with Laurel and Hardy, Charlie Chaplin, Max Sennett and Max Linder, indicates this. For Magritte the spectator as for Magritte the filmmaker, movies were entertainment. This medium did not procure for him what the act of painting did: as he stated, 'Even if I knew the rudiments of the art of cinema, I could only express my ideas through painting.' In 1956, he bought a camera with which to film the little skits he cooked up with his friends in 8 mm and super-8 mm. The forty silent films he made between 1956 and 1967 make no pretence to art. Most of the scenes are like games or improvisations, and their technical quality as films is often imperfect. They show his companions in different situations, interacting with objects from Magritte's repertoire (apple, trombone, bowler hat) or directly with the paintings. Louis Scutenaire has said, 'Magritte granted complete latitude to some and was content to film their more or less improvised sketches. But like the most implacable of directors, he sternly imposed gestures and miming on others.' The result is tinged with humour, a dreamlike atmosphere and even eroticism. The actors are recognizable, most often Magritte himself, Georgette, Louis Scutenaire, Irène Hamoir, E. L. T. Mesens and Paul Colinet. While these films may lack artistic merit, they plunge us into the artist's everyday surroundings and his Surrealist imagination, while they attest to the easy-going atmosphere that reigned among Magritte and his Brussels sidekicks.

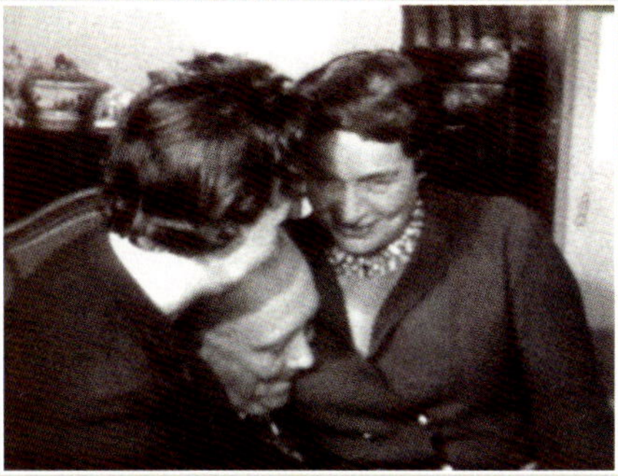

Still photo from the film *The Bookcase* by René Magritte, October–December 1956
Irène Hamoir, Louis Scutenaire and Georgette Magritte in *The Bookcase*, filmed at the artist's home, Schaerbeek (Brussels)

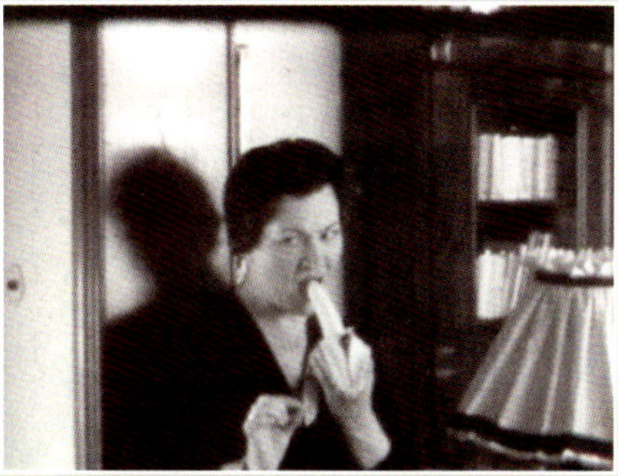

Still photo from the film *The Antillean Dessert* by René Magritte, April 1957
Irène Hamoir eating a banana

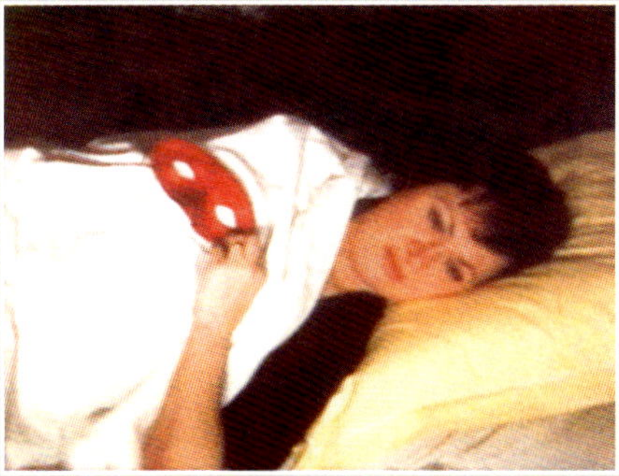

Still photo from the film *Tuba* by René Magritte, 21 November 1960
Irène Hamoir, reclining, holding a red mask

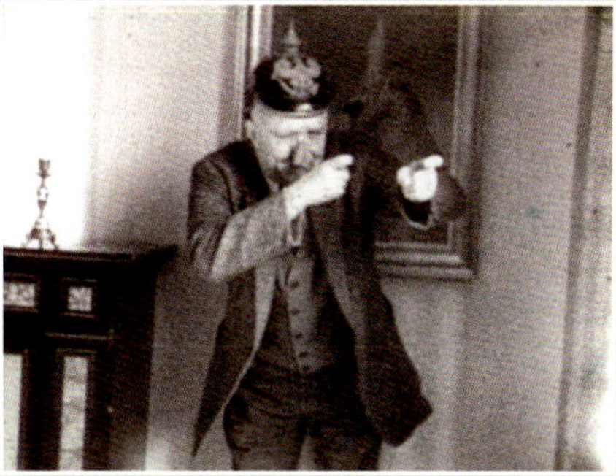

Still photo from the film *The Total Scenario* by René Magritte, October 1956–March 1957
Louis Scutenaire

The Domain of Arnheim

1962
Oil on canvas
146 x 114 cm
Inv. 10707

In a letter to Edward James, Magritte discussed a painting he was working on: 'It is "The Domain of Arnheim", in remembrance of a tale by Poe that in my opinion conjures up thoughts of this kind: mountains are moved so that the sun will appear in accordance with a determined desire.' He also said it was a vision that Poe would have appreciated. The title is from a story that was first published in 1847. Magritte, who could not read English, knew it in the translation by Baudelaire. He probably identified with the personality of Mr Ellison, the main character, whom he described as 'a poet in the broadest and noblest sense . . . and who could perhaps have been a painter'. This painting uses various recurrent themes and motifs from the artist's œuvre. The iconography of the mountain-bird whose petrified wings seem to guard a nest appeared in 1938 in the first version of *The Domain of Arnheim*. Magritte employed this characteristic petrification particularly in 1950 and 1951, when he made nineteen paintings involving the theme. Here, the pairing of day and night is combined with an uncertain atmosphere, the moon appearing in a clear sky that seems already plunged into darkness. A balustrade with an object on it (often a nest) appears frequently in the paintings. Its presence, enhanced here by the work's monumentality, invites viewers to immerse themselves, to lean their elbows on it, dive into this world and become the lone witness of this supernatural wonder. While this image was produced in several variants, the version bequeathed to the Royal Museums of Fine Arts of Belgium by Georgette Magritte is the most majestic.

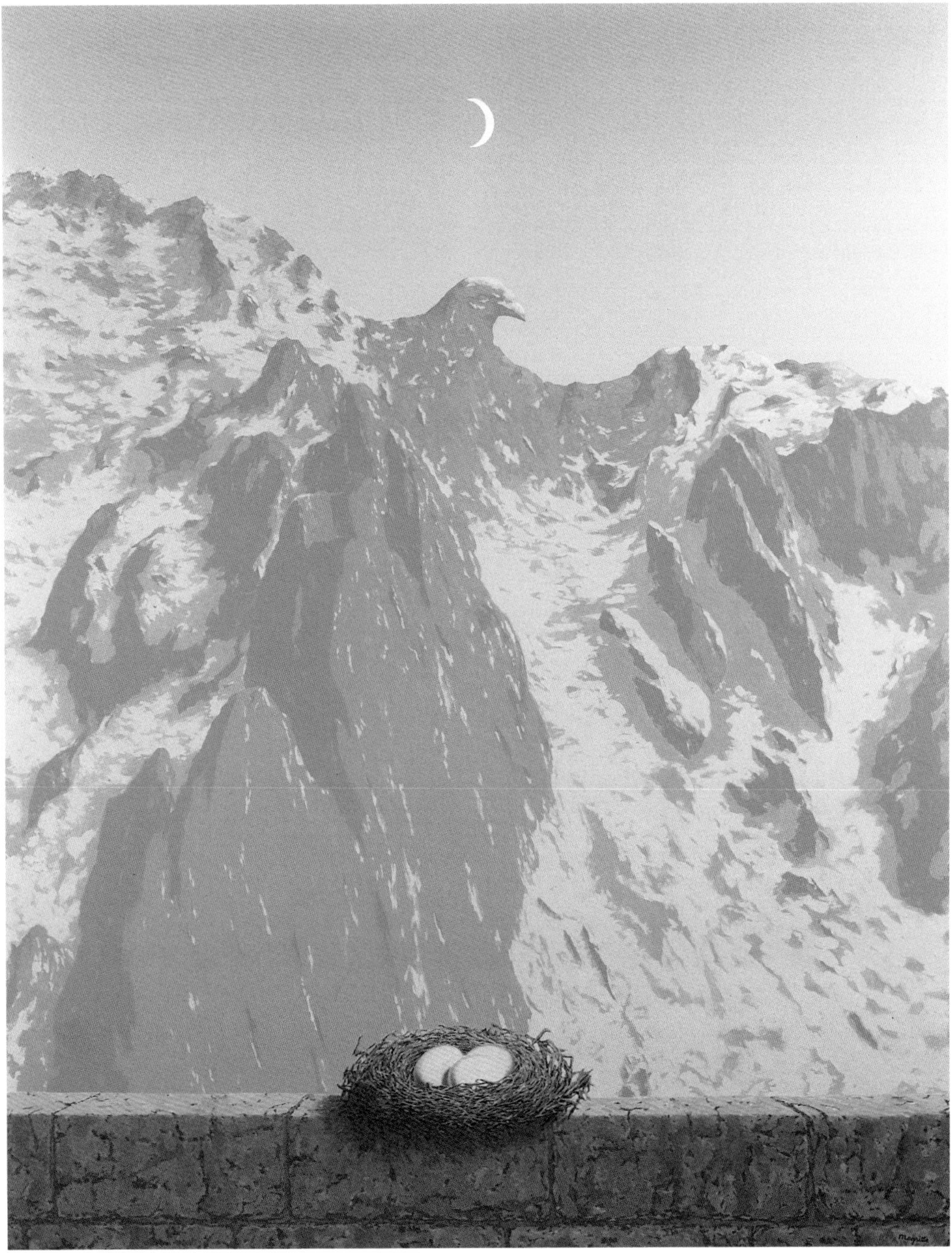

THE SEARCH FOR TRUTH

1963
Oil on canvas
130.5 x 97.2 cm
Inv. 7008

The Search for Truth was acquired by the Royal Museums of Fine Arts in 1963 at the request of its chief curator, Philippe Roberts-Jones. In a letter to the Minister of National Education and Culture justifying the acquisition of this work, Roberts-Jones wrote, 'There is no need to emphasize the pre-eminence of René Magritte not only in the Belgian school but also internationally, as he is considered one of the most influential figures of the Surrealist movement. Unfortunately, he is still quite inadequately represented in our collection. For a number of years, we have been trying to fill this gap but have encountered tremendous difficulties because the painter was bound by contract to a New York gallery that took all his production. *The Search for Truth* is a canvas Magritte executed expressly for the Museum of Modern Art in Brussels, at my request and by special agreement.' It is the fourth work of Magritte purchased by the Royal Museums and the second commissioned directly from him, after *The Dominion of Light* in 1954. It brings together well-known elements of Magritte's vocabulary. The sleigh bell, which is traditionally hung around a horse's neck, appeared for the first time in 1926 in *The Silvered Chasm* and is probably the object that recurs the most frequently, no doubt because of its adaptability, as David Sylvester has pointed out. The window opening onto a blue sky with clouds and a seascape is also found in many paintings. The vertical fish appeared three years earlier in *The Presence of Mind*. Magritte combines these diverse elements into a surprising, even perplexing whole: 'In so far as my paintings are valid, they do not lend themselves to analysis.'

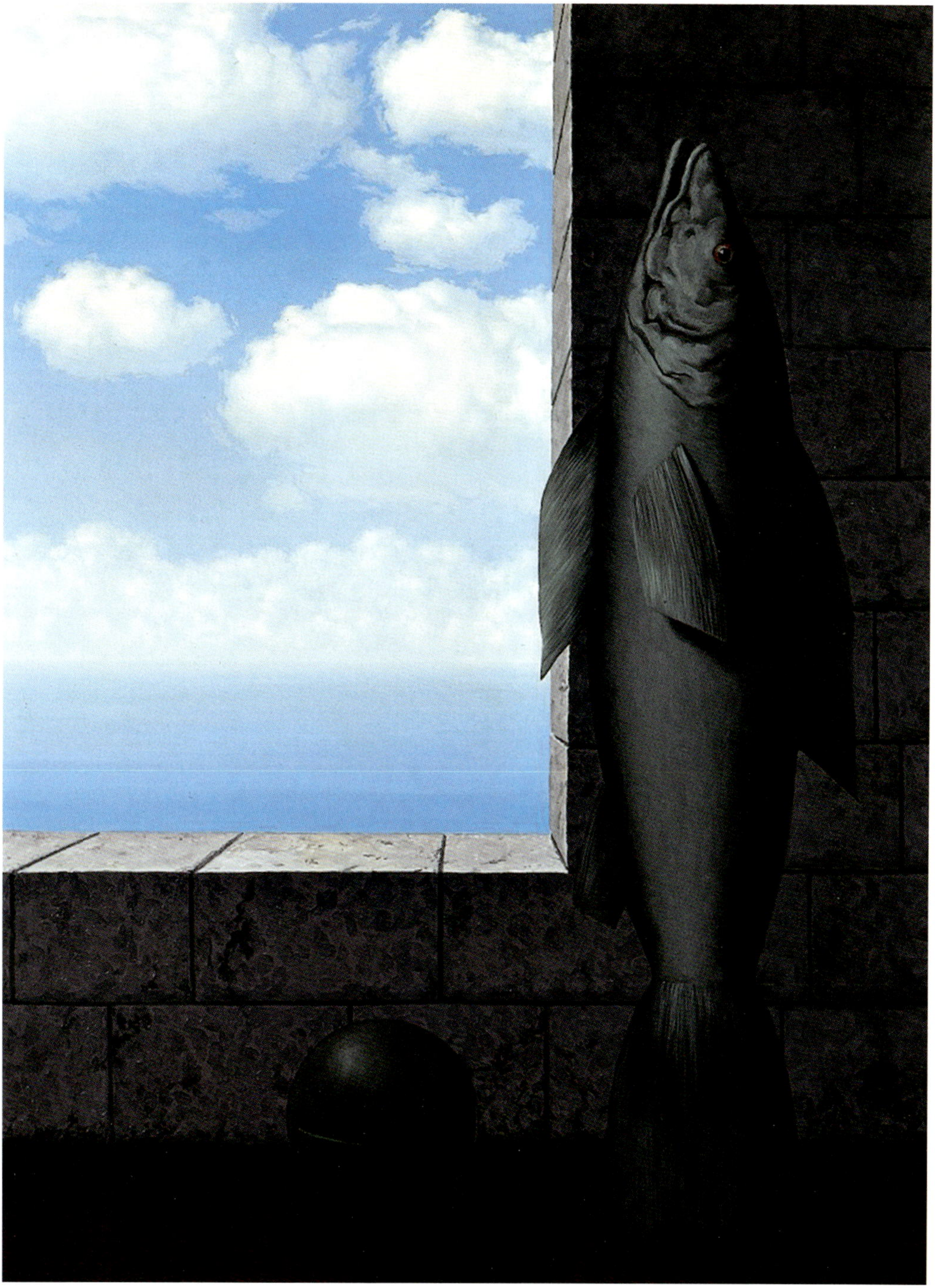

The Blank Page

1967
Oil on canvas
54 x 65 cm
Inv. 10711

According to Georgette Magritte, *The Blank Page* is the last work Magritte completed before his death in 1967. Soon after, Charles Flamand, who used the pseudonym Carl Waï, published an account of a conversation he had had with the artist about this work not long before. Upon asking Waï and a young girl to describe the canvas, Magritte realized that what they saw did not correspond to what he had meant to depict. The two young people insisted that the quarter moon was *behind* the leaves. 'Then I have failed,' Magritte declared, 'because I tried to put the leaves behind the moon.' Magritte consequently changed the quarter moon into a full moon to eliminate any ambiguity. And when the young girl expressed her enthusiasm for a moon hidden by leaves, Magritte answered, 'I too like to see leaves hiding the moon. But if you saw leaves behind the moon, that would be unheard-of: life would at last have meaning!' The depiction of a heavenly body blocking out foliage is first seen in 1957, in *The Banquet*, but in that instance, it is the sun.

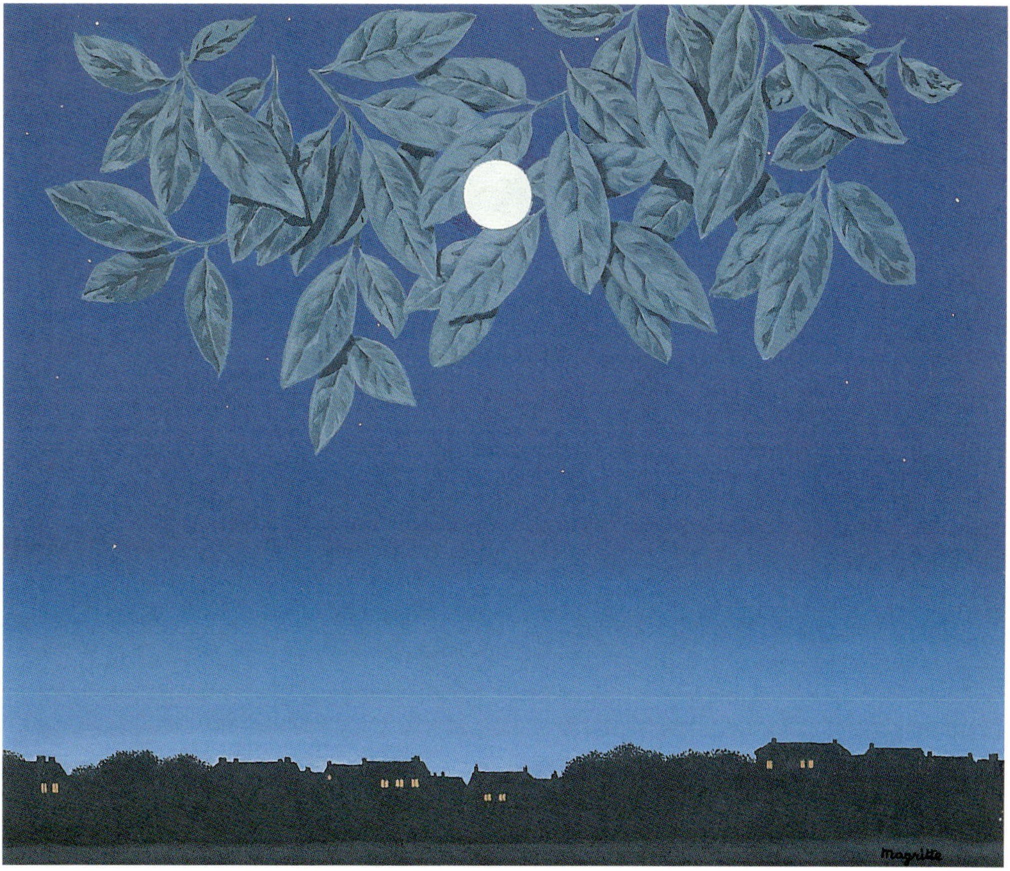
Magritte

– 3 –

A DYNAMIC INSTALLATION OF WORKS ON LOAN

This section pays tribute to the many lenders whose support and generosity have continuously enriched the museum with major and lesser-known works, all of which are essential to understanding the artistic production of René Magritte as a whole.
This selection, which represents one-fifth of the works lent to the museum since it opened in 2009, illustrates the dynamic nature of an installation that seeks to constantly rethink itself in order to enable the public to discover new masterpieces at every visit.

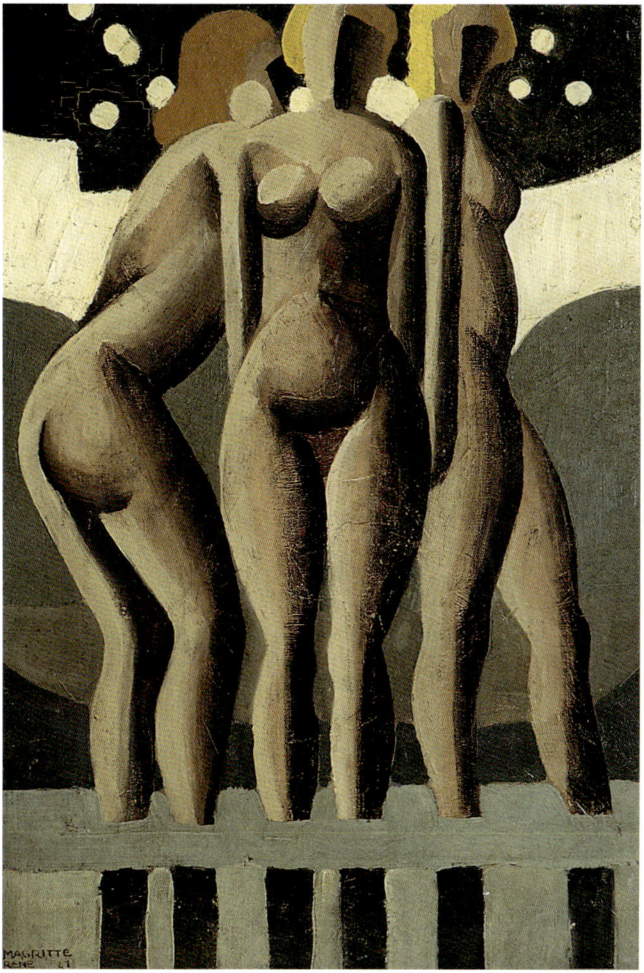

This early work shows the Cubist orientation of Magritte's initial years. At the time, the female nude was the favoured vehicle for experiments in painting.

Bathers
1921
Oil on canvas
55 x 38 cm
Collection Université libre de Bruxelles, Brussels

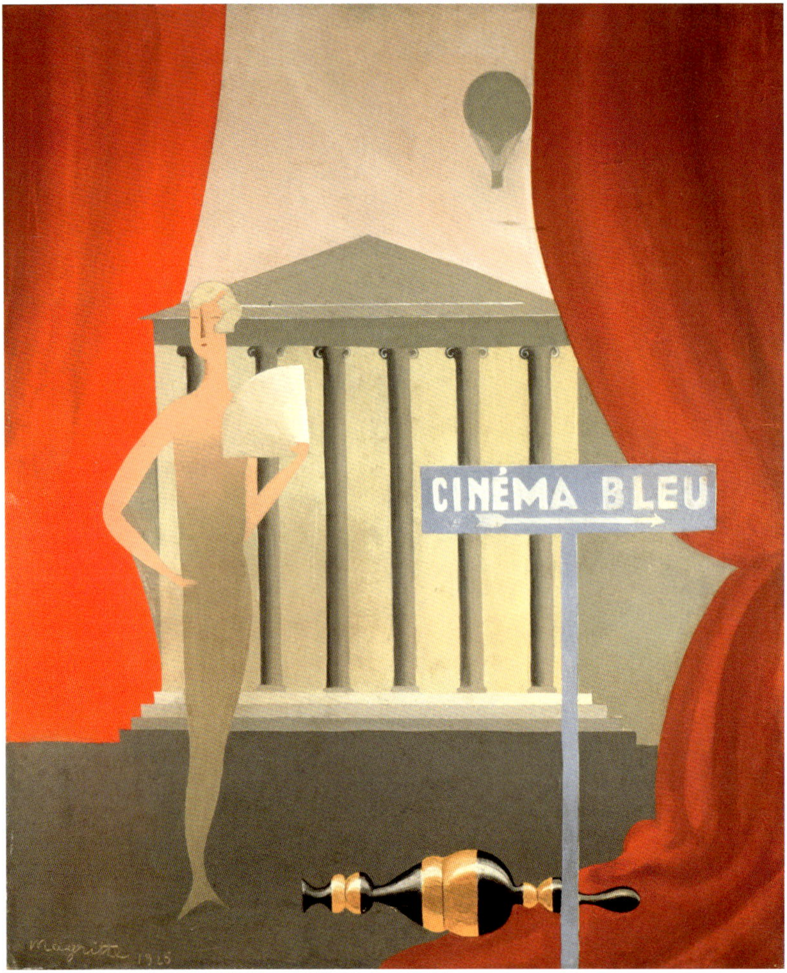

Cinéma bleu is the name of the theatre in Charleroi where Magritte often went to the movies in his youth. The red curtain, bilboquet and hot-air balloon in this canvas herald some elements of Magritte's later repertoire. The woman, with her short hair and long, slender figure, is a Roaring Twenties flapper. She recalls the illustrations Magritte drew for sheet-music covers around the same time.

Cinéma bleu [Blue Cinema]
1925
Oil on canvas
65 x 54 cm
Collection Nahmad, Switzerland

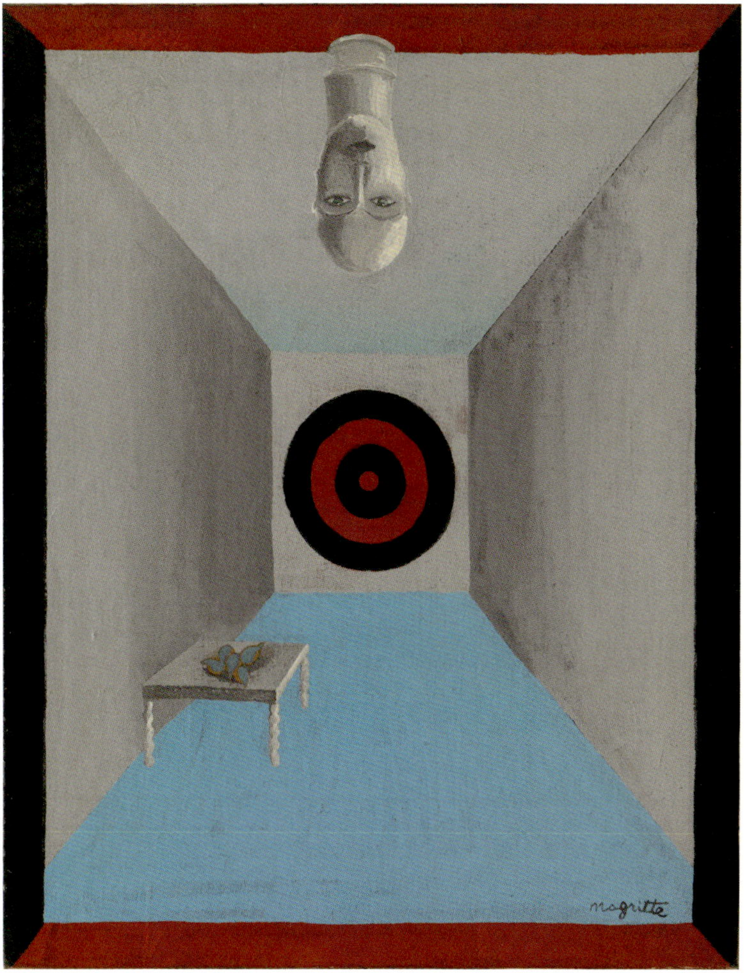

The garish palette of this atypical work resembles neither the autumnal colours of the early years nor the sombre tones of the 'Cavernous' period. It is a one-of-a-kind composition that Magritte never repeated.

The Shooting Gallery
1926
Oil and enamel paint on canvas
77 x 63 cm
Private collection

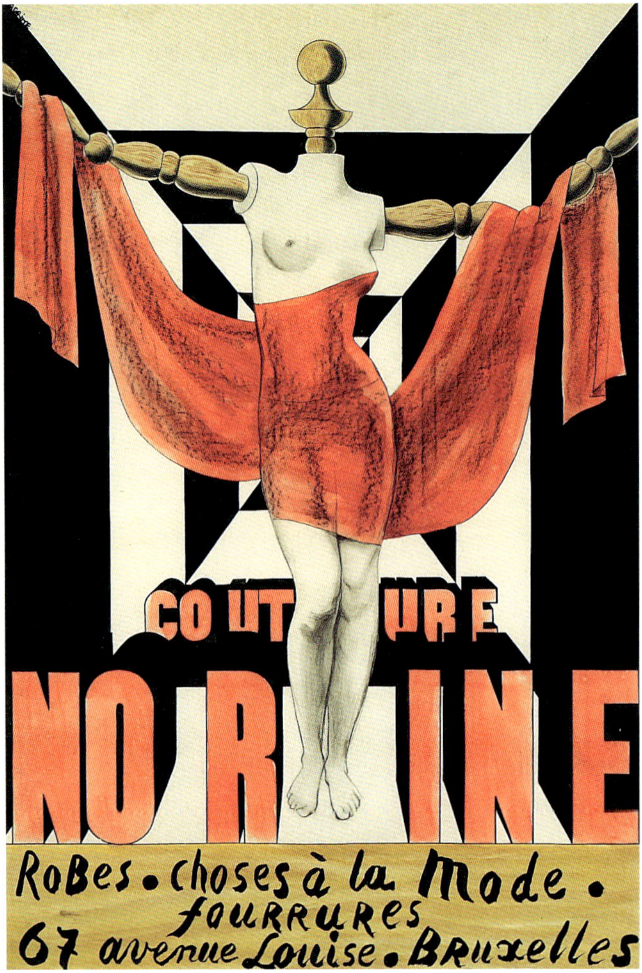

Magritte first worked for the fashion design firm Norine in 1924. Its director, Honorine Deschrijver, was the wife of Paul-Gustave van Hecke, Magritte's first dealer. The artist's personal Surrealist vocabulary begins to take shape here in the bilboquet, woman's breasts and red drape.

Couture Norine
Poster design
1926
Gouache, pencil, brush and ink on paper
117.5 x 80.6 cm
Private collection, courtesy Guggenheim Asher Associates, Inc., New York

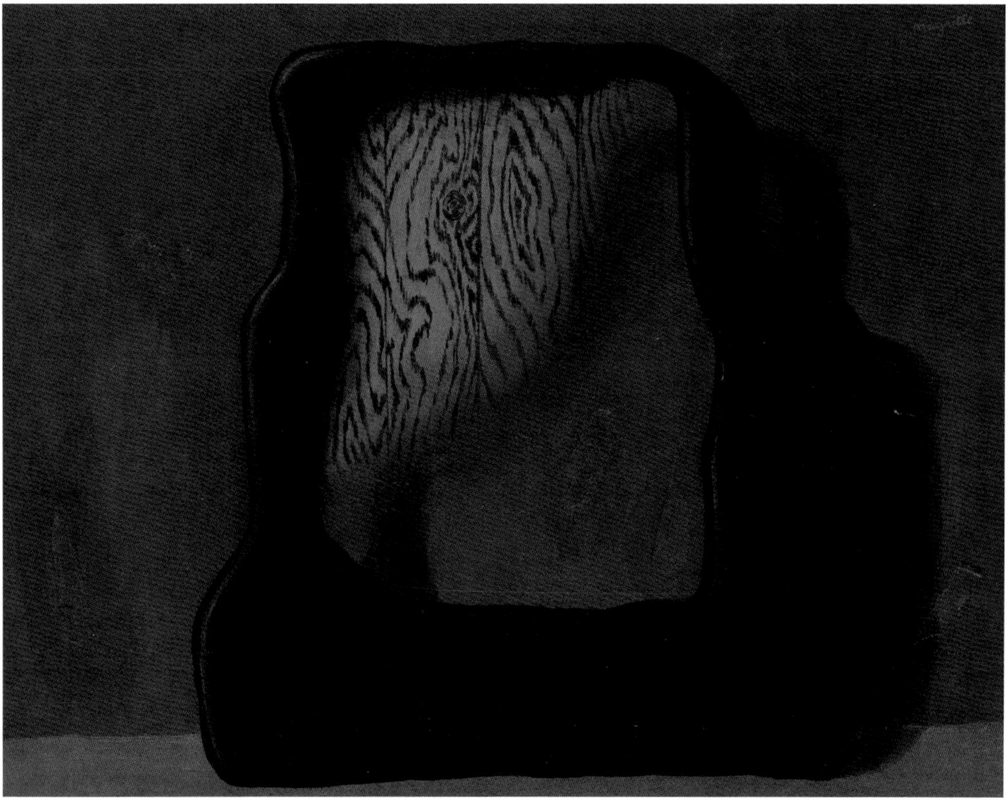

'I have found a new potential in things: for them to *gradually* become something else . . . Some planks of good wood imperceptibly become transparent in places.' As in *The Imp of the Perverse* (1928), the iconography here is distinctive for the process of metamorphosis, also used in other works from the same period. This is furthermore one of the few examples of collage in the artist's output: patches are visible on the surface of the painting.

The Prince of Objects
1927
Collage and oil on canvas
50 x 65 cm
Private collection,
courtesy Galerie Vedovi, Brussels

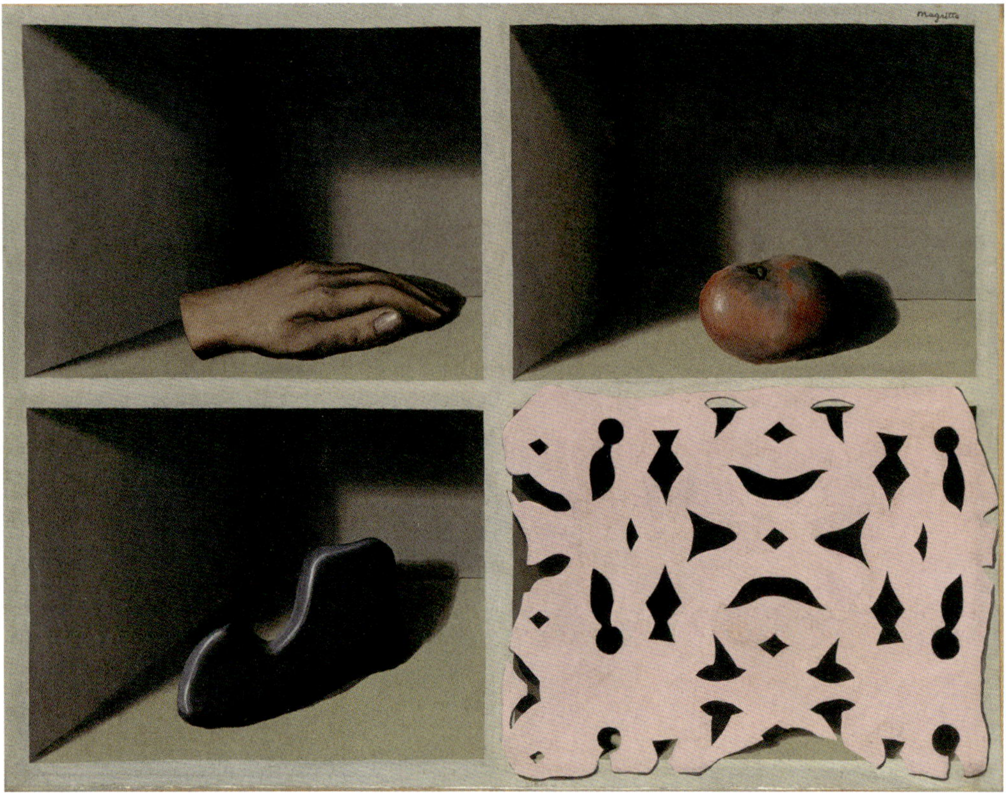

Compartmentalization – distributing objects in pigeon-holes – was a classic feature of the 'word paintings' (for example, *The Interpretation of Dreams*, 1927), in which image and text are combined in a new relationship. In 1959, when Magritte was making gouache variants for the Chicago collector Barnet Hodes, he revisited this painting: the head of a bird, a sleigh bell, a stemmed glass filled with water and a pigeon-hole hidden by a paper cut-out are the objects represented in that version.

One-night Museum
1927
Oil on canvas
50 x 65 cm
Private collection, London

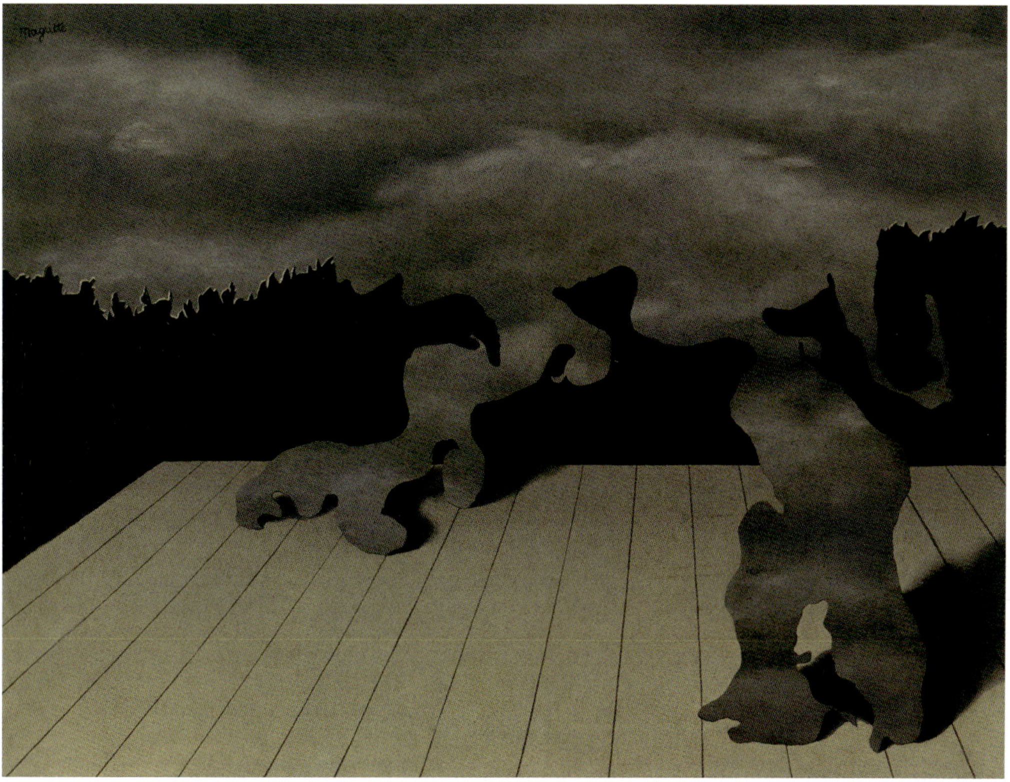

Magritte described this work in a letter to Paul Nougé: 'The legs of the sky. – The floor lit by the moon, which we know is behind us, is not surrounded by walls – it and some distant trees hide an area of sky. But a section of the floor is in turn hidden by the sky's legs, which are standing on it and cannot be the occasion for futile thoughts.'

The Muscles of the Sky
1927
Oil on canvas
54 x 73 cm
Private collection

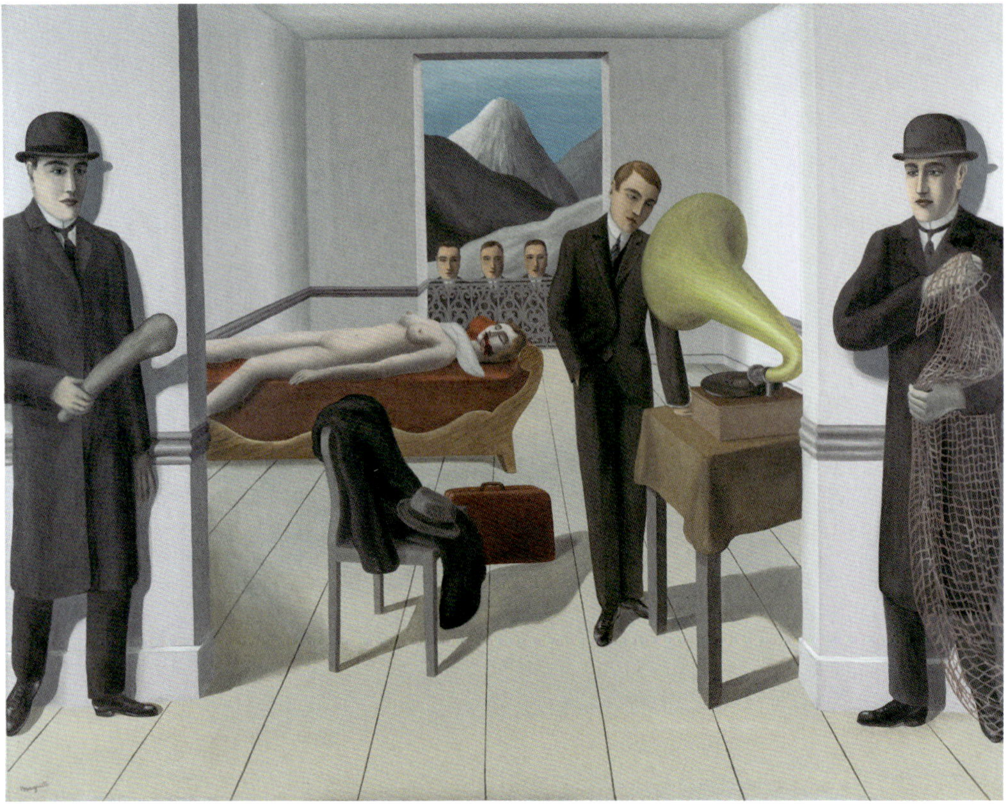

This work, which forms a diptych with *The Secret Player*, is emblematic of the dark world and anguished atmosphere reigning in Magritte's compositions at that time. Drawing upon a poem from Paul Nougé's *Les Images peintes* (1927), a scene from a Fantômas movie directed by Louis Feuillade and a painting by Max Ernst – *The Virgin Chastises the Infant Jesus before Three Witnesses* – Magritte created one of the masterpieces of his 'Dark' period.

The Menaced Assassin
1927
Oil on canvas
152 x 195 cm
The Museum of Modern Art, New York.
Kay Sage Tanguy Fund

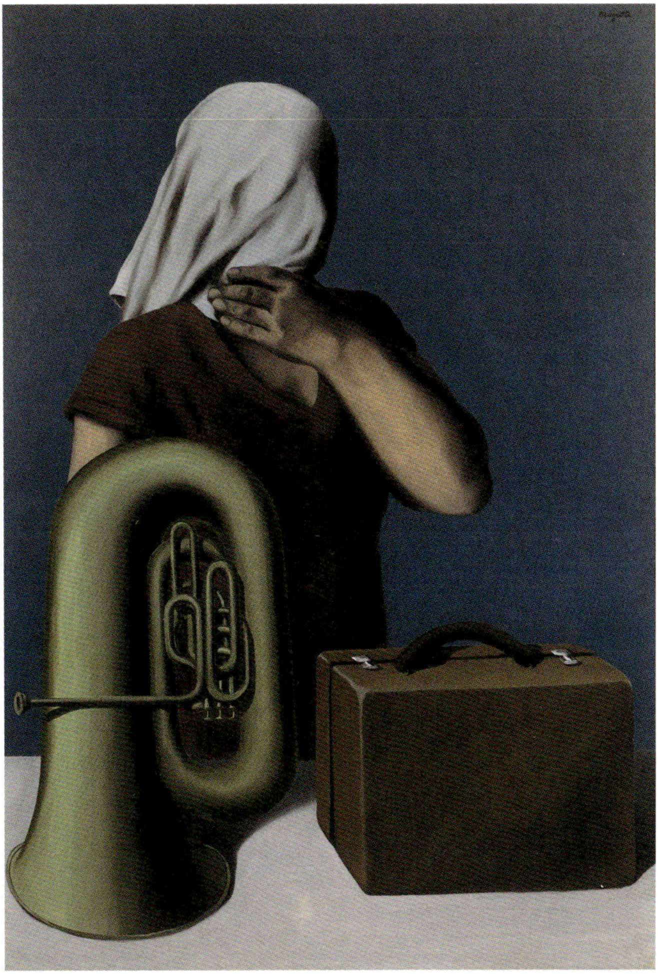

The iconography of this canvas may be derived from the cover of the thirty-fifth episode of *Nick Carter, le grand détective américain*. The young Magritte was an avid reader of the adventures of the American 'master detective'. The cover represents a woman lying on her back, obviously dead, her face covered with a cloth. The motif of the veiled face occurs many other times in Magritte's œuvre. Some interpret it as the memory of a childhood trauma: his mother drowned herself in the River Sambre. When the body was discovered, her face was covered by her nightgown.

The Central Story
1928
Oil on canvas
116 x 81 cm
Collection Belfius Banque & Assurances

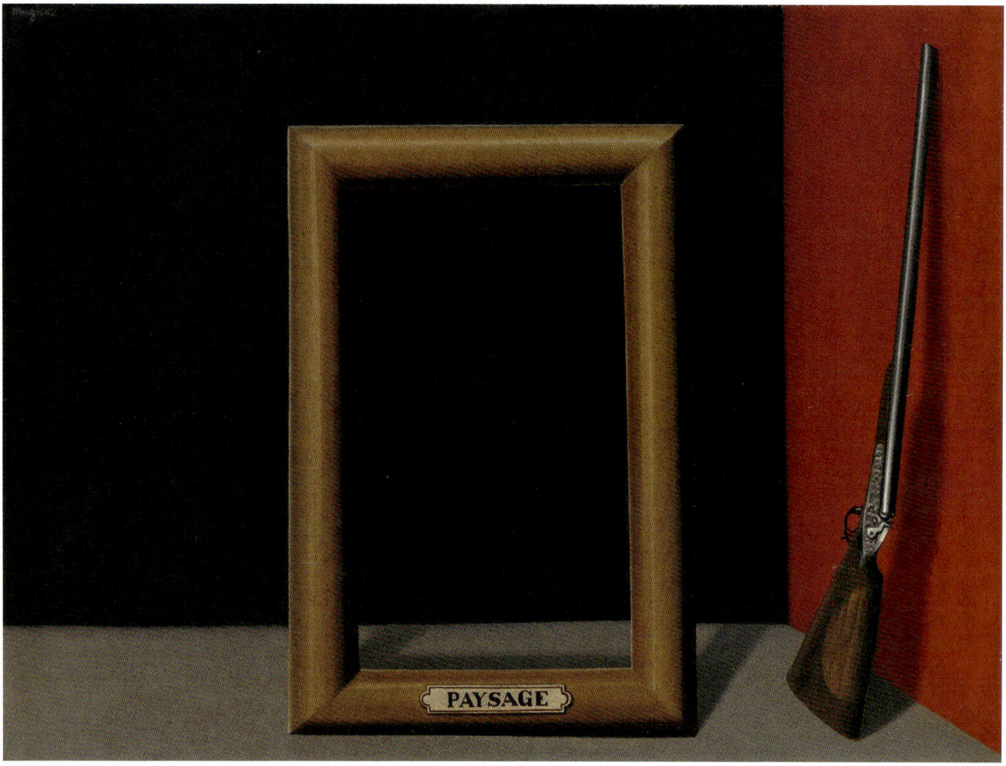

The Delights of Landscape
1928
Oil on canvas
54 x 73 cm
Private collection, London

Magritte took his inspiration from a passage in Edgar Allan Poe's 'The Pit and the Pendulum' (1842), which he read in Baudelaire's translation: 'It was not that I feared to look upon things horrible, but that I grew aghast lest there should be nothing to see.' The invisible, the hidden, the prohibition on seeing and the vision of 'nothing' are leitmotifs in Magritte's work, attesting to the interest Surrealists showed in the sense of sight.

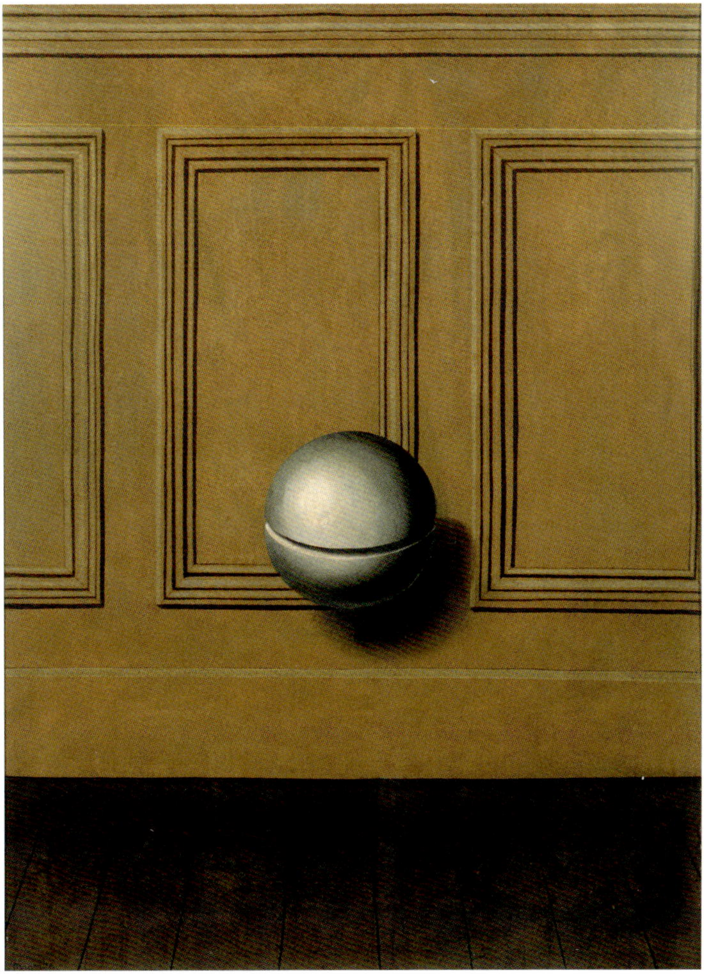

Probably dating from Magritte's time in Paris, this painting depicts the motif of the sleigh bell, one of Magritte's most frequent motifs. He depicted it in a range of forms, including a variant similar to *The Automaton* in which it rests on a chair cushion.

The Automaton
1929
Oil on canvas
73 x 54 cm
Private collection, Belgium

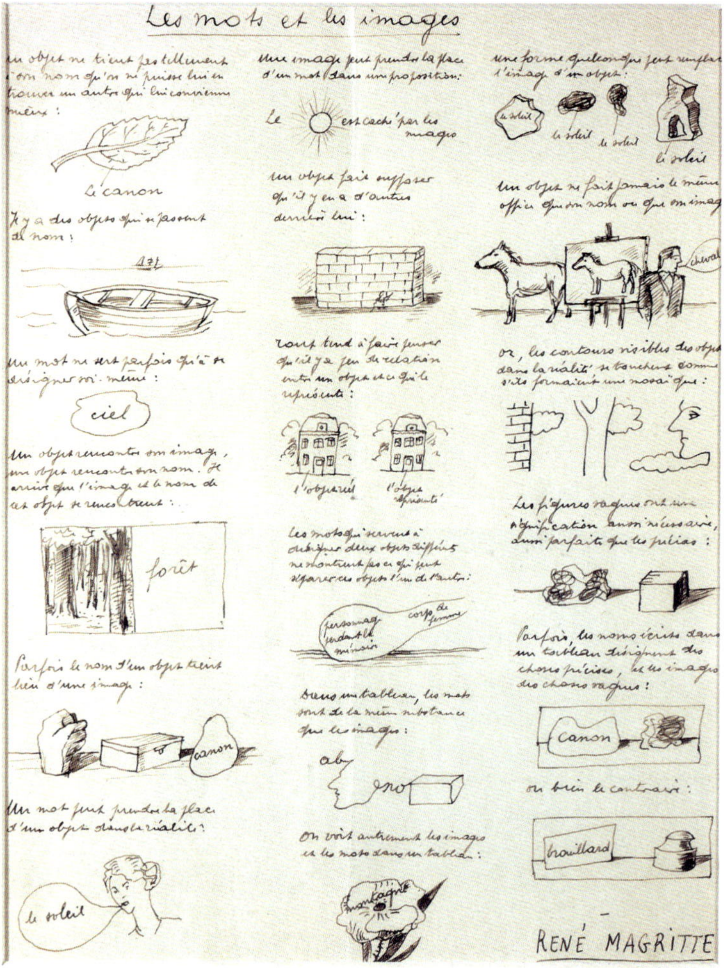

Published in 1929 in the twelfth issue of the Paris magazine *La Révolution surréaliste*, 'Words and Images' postulates a set of possible relationships between the word and the image. Magritte had begun putting these ideas into practice in 1927 with his first 'word paintings', a concept he developed in many works during his years in Paris.

Words and Images
1929
Indian ink on paper
27.5 x 21.2 cm
Page published in *La Révolution surréaliste*, no. 12, 15 December 1929
Patronage AG Insurance

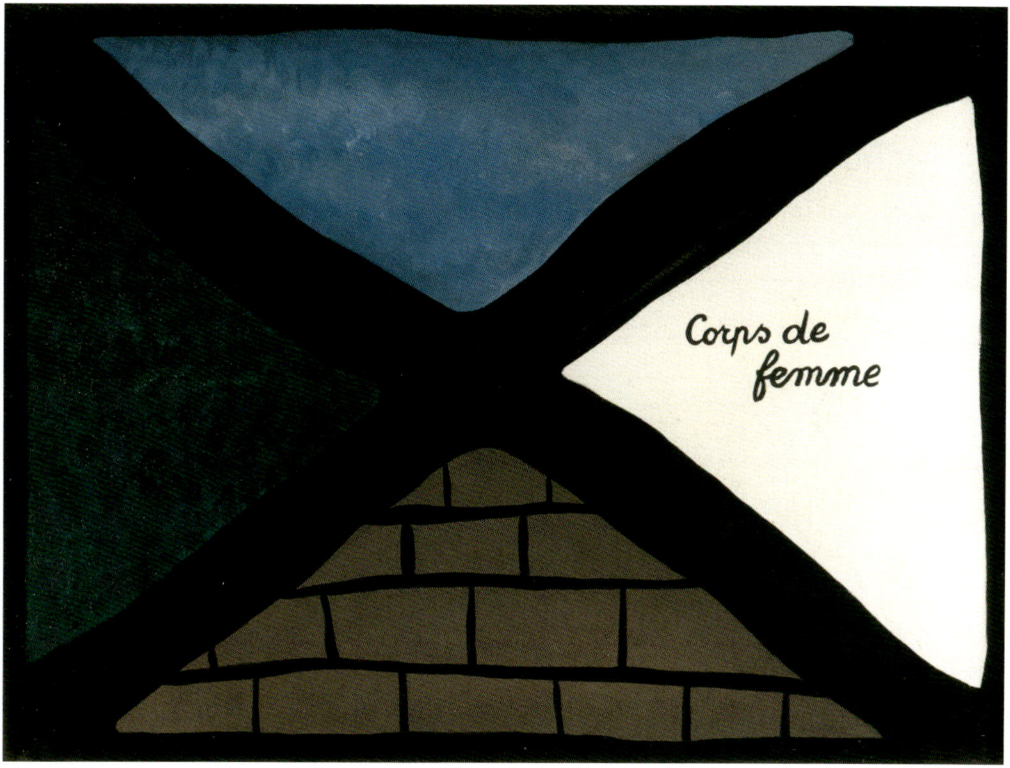

The composition of this canvas is unique, although the idea of compartments was not new. It illustrates the postulate from 'Words and Images' in which Magritte states: 'Sometimes, the names written in a picture designate precise things, while the images are vague.'

The Literal Meaning
1929
Oil on canvas
54 x 73 cm
Private collection, courtesy Galerie Maurice Keitelman

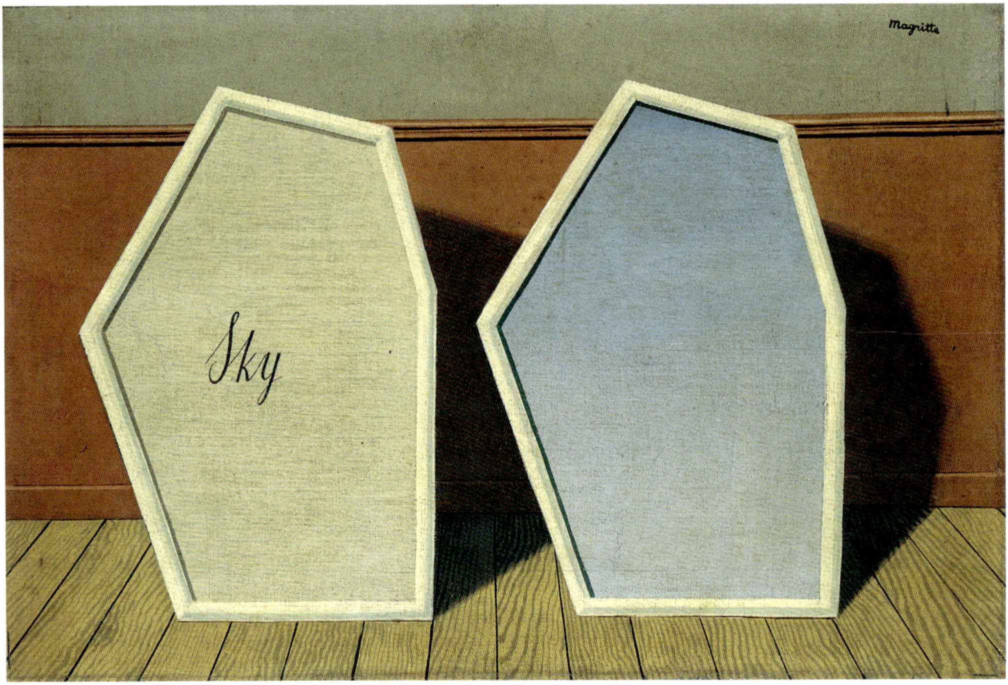

The Palace of Curtains is one of Magritte's 'word paintings'. The use of English here attests to an opening onto the international market and Magritte's wish to reach a foreign audience. This work was exhibited in New York in 1936 at Magritte's first solo show at the Julien Levy Gallery.

The Palace of Curtains
1935
Oil on canvas mounted on wood
27 x 41 cm
Collection Pierre Alechinsky

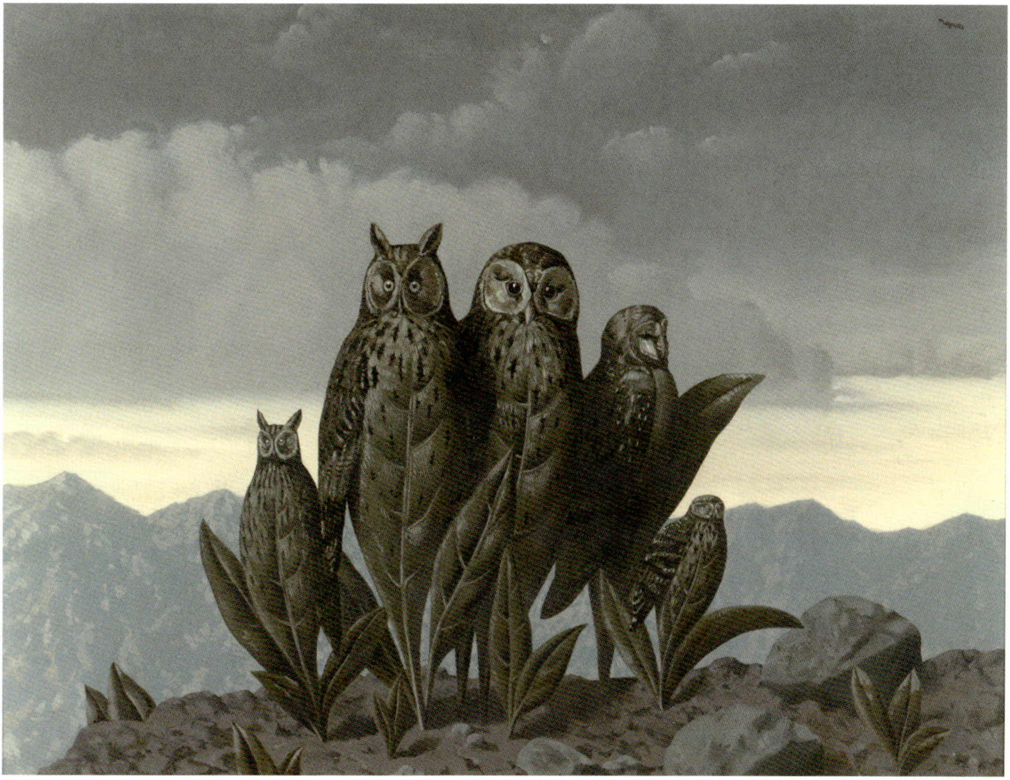

This is one of three variants of *The Companions of Fear*. The Royal Museums of Fine Arts owns a gouache version.

The Companions of Fear
1942
Oil on canvas
70.5 x 92 cm
Private collection

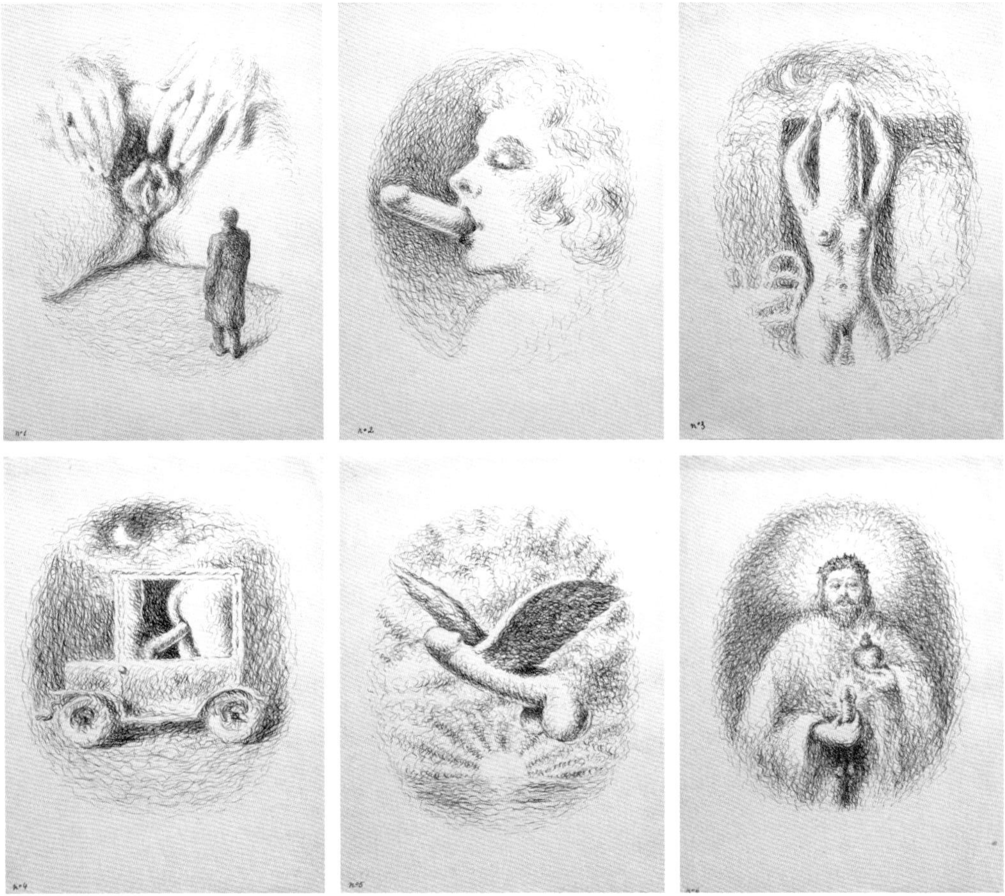

6 erotic drawings for a novel by Georges Bataille
1946
Pencil and ink on paper
No. 1: 35.4 x 25.3 cm
No. 2: 35.4 x 25.3 cm
No. 3: 35.6 x 25.3 cm
No. 4: 35.8 x 25.3 cm
No. 5: 35.8 x 25.3 cm
No. 6: 35.6 x 25.3 cm
Private collection

These drawings were done in 1946 to illustrate a new edition of the French author Georges Bataille's erotic novel *Madame Edwarda* but were never published. They were presented in the exhibition *Magritte retrouvé* at the Magritte Museum in 2012.

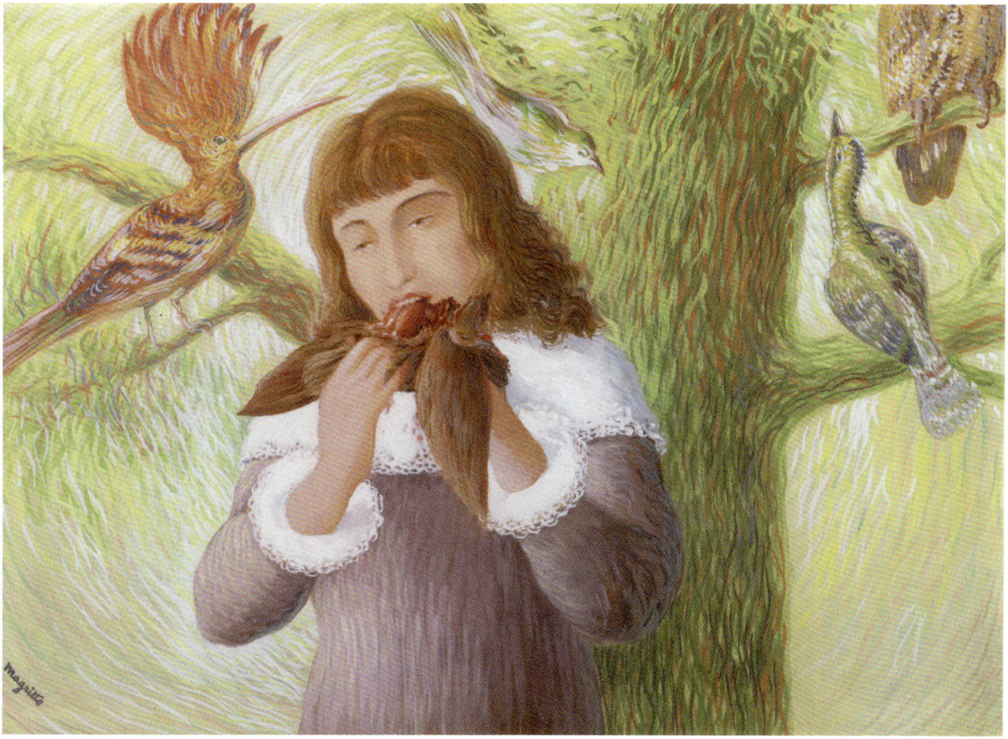

Also known as *Girl Eating a Bird*, this work has an unsettling iconography that is further emphasized by a title like *Pleasure*. It corresponds to a scenario written by Paul Nougé in *Les Images peintes* (1927): 'It is then that we surprise the pallor of joy, eyelids drawn open onto the cruelty of dreams, teeth braced against the lips' blood, a woman withdrawn into her pleasure, who savours, through the caress of the feathers, a docile creature never to cease living.'

Pleasure
1946
Gouache on paper
36 x 49.5 cm
Collection Lucien Bilinelli, Brussels

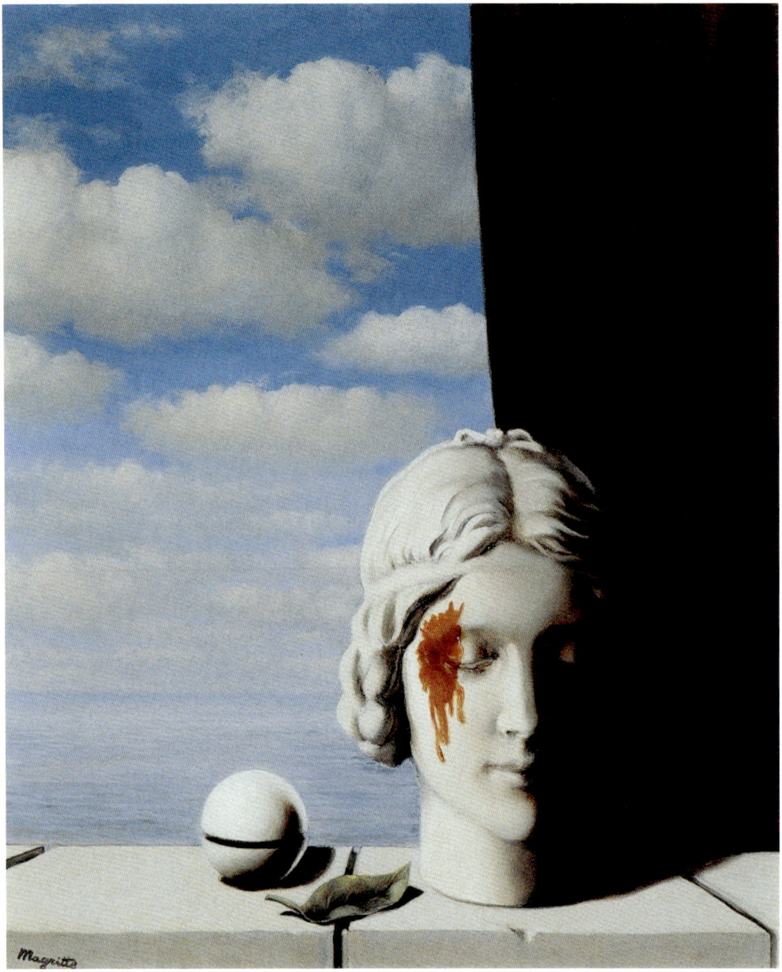

This plaster head, of which Magritte purchased several copies at Maison Berger, appears in a number of his works, including blue-painted sculptures of a woman's head. Its depiction in the paintings might also be a recollection of Giorgio de Chirico's *Song of Love*, which features an antique head. If elements of the composition – balustrade, sleigh bell, red curtain, seascape – recall other works, the disturbing bloodstain on this woman's strangely serene face infuses the scene with drama.

Memory
1948
Oil on canvas
60 x 50 cm
Property of the Belgian State

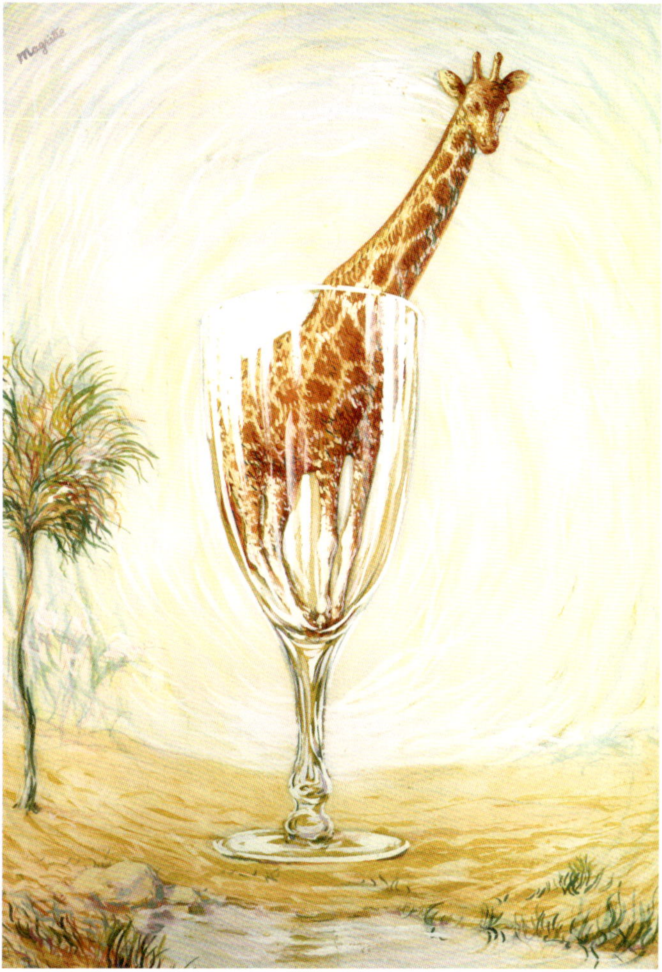

‘In an enchanting desert light, a giraffe appears in a large crystal glass.’ This description, provided by Magritte himself, draws attention to the play on proportions that is a common feature of his work. *The Heartstring* (1960) is another example of an enlarged glass in a landscape. From a stylistic point of view, this gouache shows the brush handling typical of ‘Surrealism in Full Sunlight’, with its luminous tones and energetic, swirling touch.

The Cut-glass Bath
1949
Gouache on paper
46 x 36 cm
Collection Eclipse, London

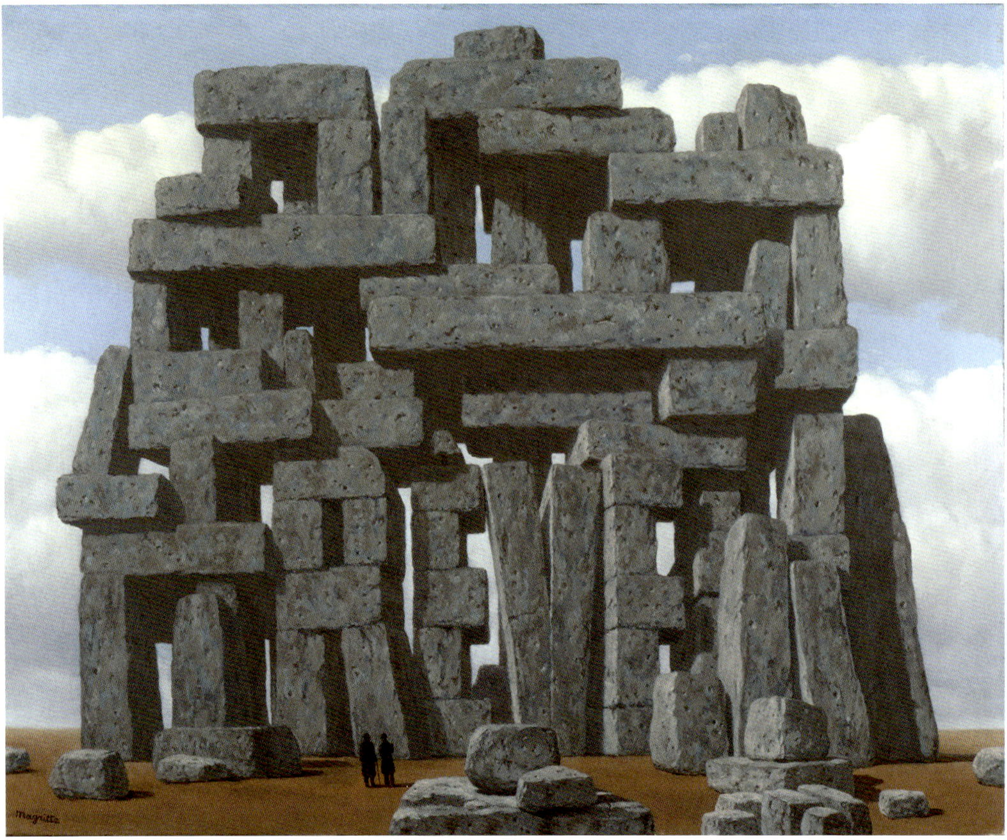

The Art of Conversation is from a series of paintings all having the same title in which 'a word sometimes serves only to designate itself' ('Words and Images'). The iconographic choice here refers to Baudelaire's poem 'Beauty', from the collection *The Flowers of Evil* (1857), which begins, 'I'm fair, O mortals, as a dream of stone.' The painting is also an example from the period during which Magritte was experimenting with petrification.

The Art of Conversation
1950
Oil on canvas
65 x 81 cm
Private collection, Switzerland

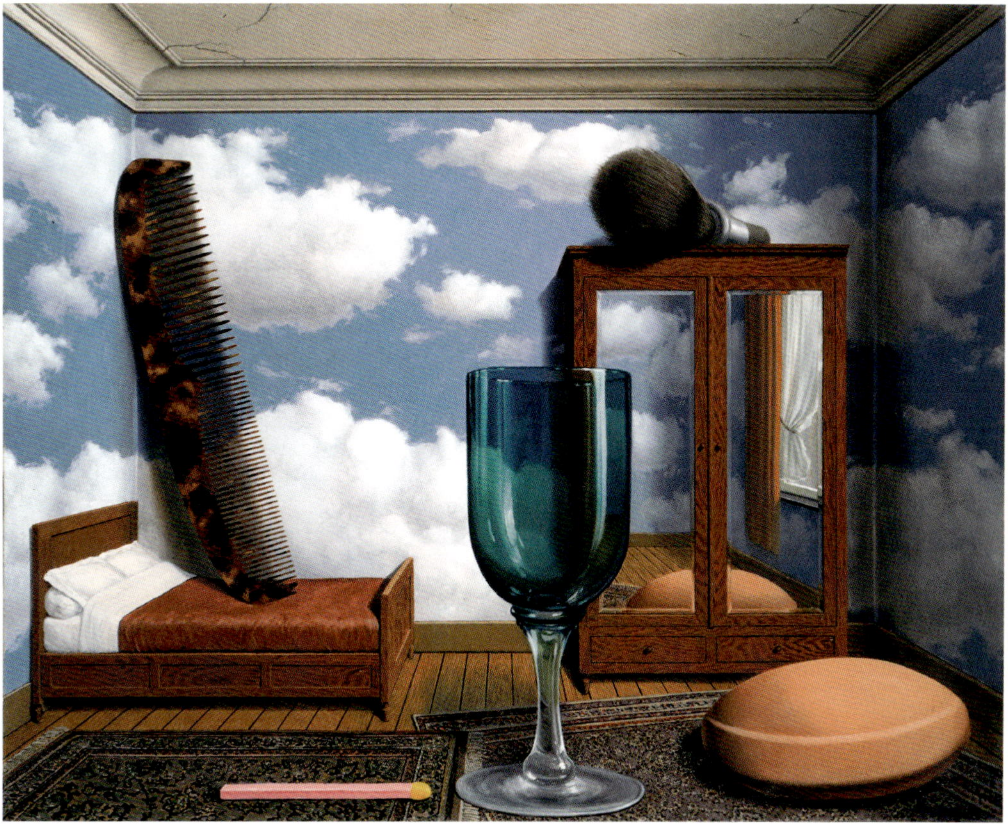

This meticulously executed work, originally entitled *Le Champ libre*, is a prime example of the theme of hypertrophied objects. It is also emblematic of the relationship that bound Magritte to the United States: in 1952, Magritte offered it to Alexander Iolas. There ensued an exchange of letters discussing such matters as the 'explanation' of an artwork and Americans' predilection for some paintings and indifference to others.

Personal Values
1952
Oil on canvas
80 x 100 cm
Collection San Francisco Museum of Modern Art. Gift Phyllis Wattis

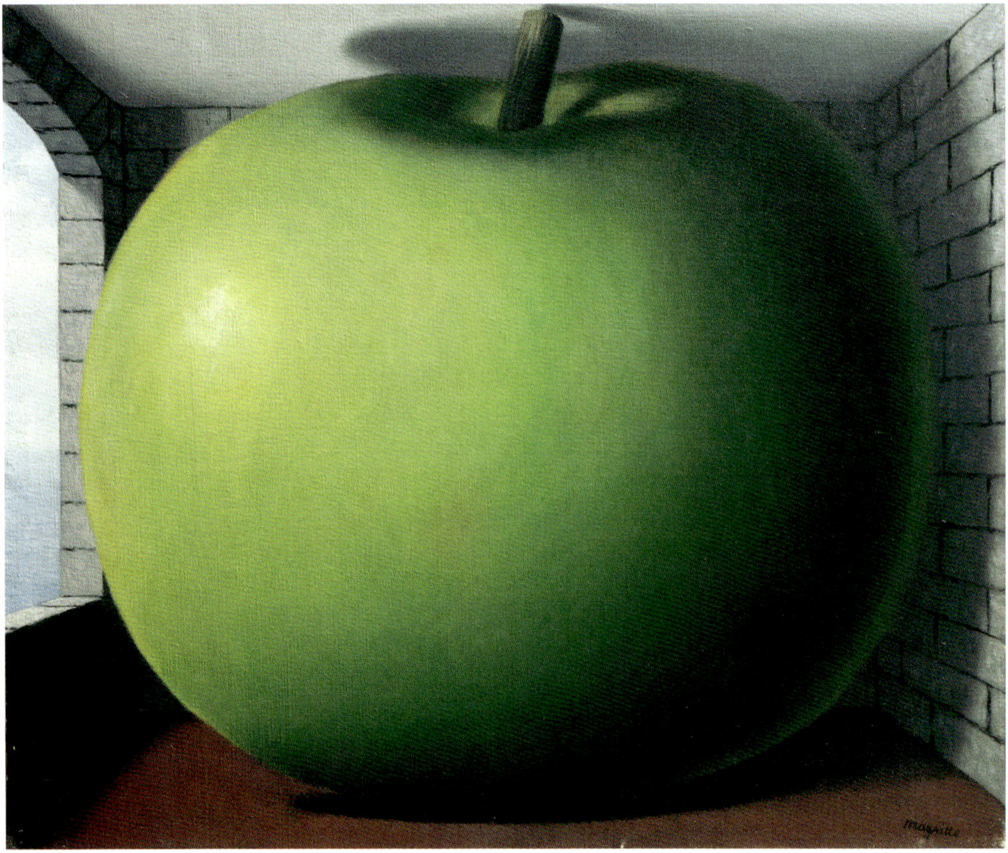

The central theme of *The Listening Room*, painted shortly after *Personal Values*, is also overgrown objects. In this image, where 'a green apple fills almost the entire space of a room', hypertrophy is pushed to the limit. Magritte reused this composition in 1960 for *The Tomb of the Wrestlers*, replacing the apple with a huge red rose.

The Listening Room
1952
Oil on canvas
45 x 55 cm
The Menil Collection, Houston

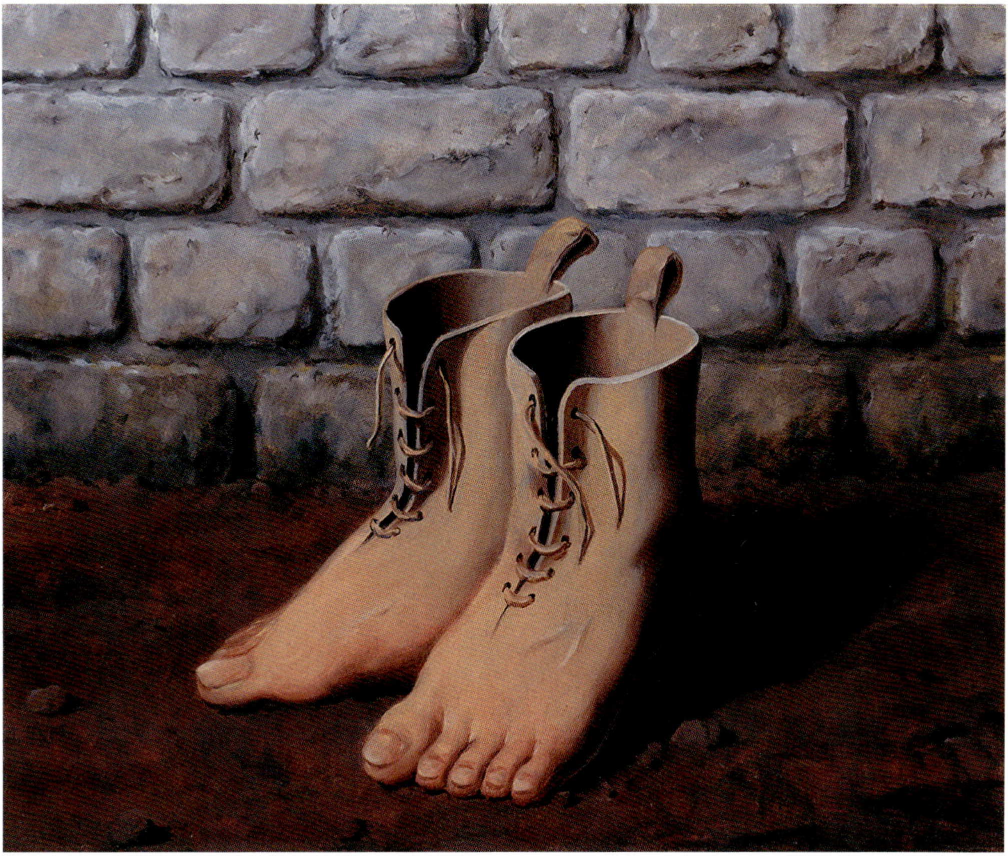

Adhering to the principle of 'elective affinities', *The Red Model* solves the problem of shoes. This problem, Magritte explains, 'demonstrates how, by force of habit, the most barbaric things easily pass for being entirely appropriate. Thanks to the "Red Model", one feels that, in reality, the union of a human foot and a leather shoe is the result of a monstrous custom.' This surprising encounter emphasizes the pre-ordained link between foot and shoe.

The Red Model
1953
Oil on canvas
38 x 46 cm
Collection BNP Paribas Fortis Bank

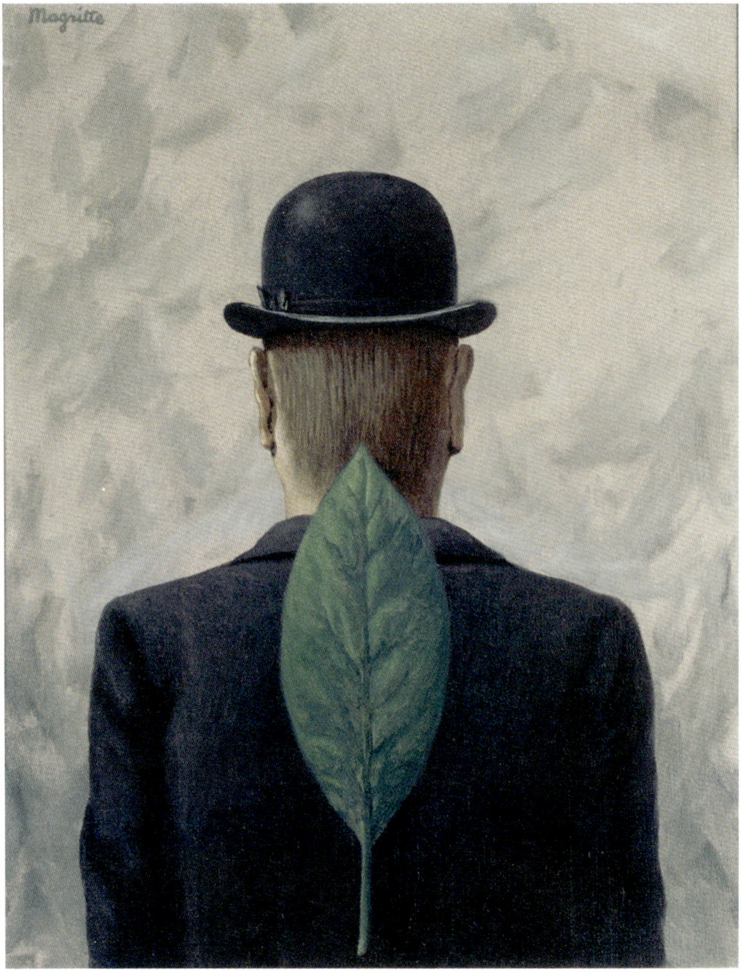

The Cultivation of Ideas could belong to the series 'La Place au soleil', which Magritte undertook in 1956, superimposing two images. The pile-up of visual information emphasizes the difference between the apparent visible and the hidden visible, a reflection underlying many works by Magritte.

The Cultivation of Ideas
1956
Oil on canvas
65 x 50 cm
Private collection

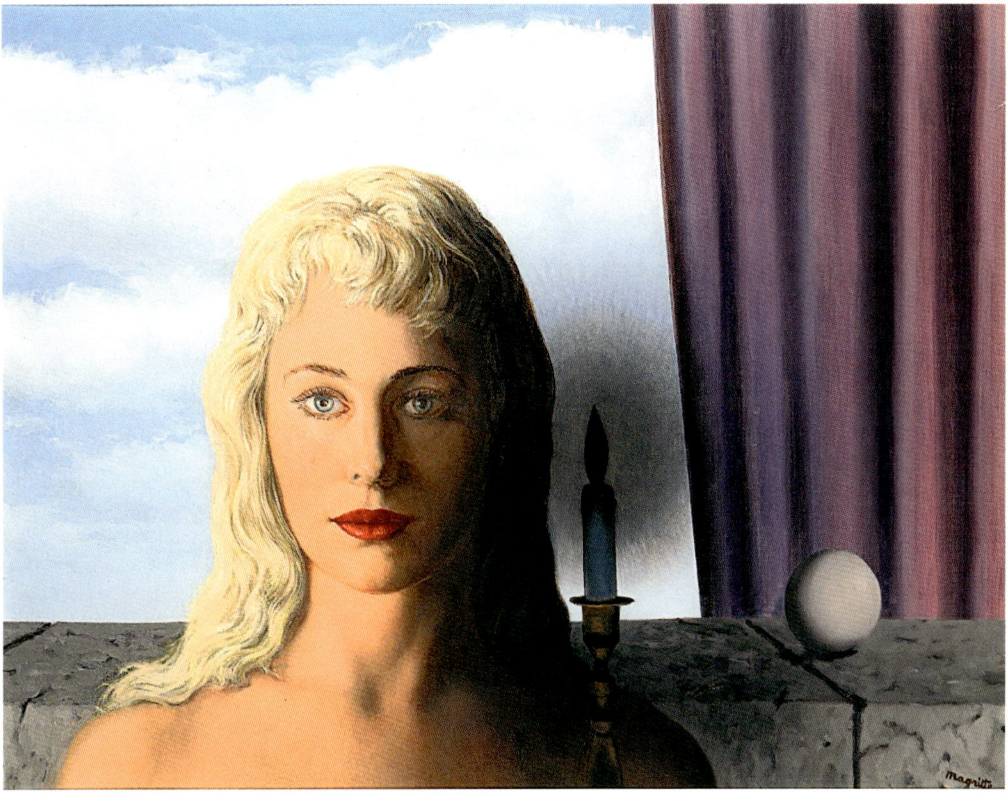

Magritte made several portraits of Anne-Marie Crowet. In this one, which reuses such classic elements from the vocabulary of his paintings as a sphere and a red curtain at the right, a troubling detail has been added: Magritte came up with *The Ignorant Fairy*, 'where we see a black candle-flame that darkens a face'. *The Ignorant Fairy* is also the title of a 1957 mural at the Palais des Beaux-Arts of Charleroi.

The Ignorant Fairy
or Portrait of Anne-Marie Crowet
1956
Oil on canvas
50 x 65 cm
Collection Baronne Gillion Crowet

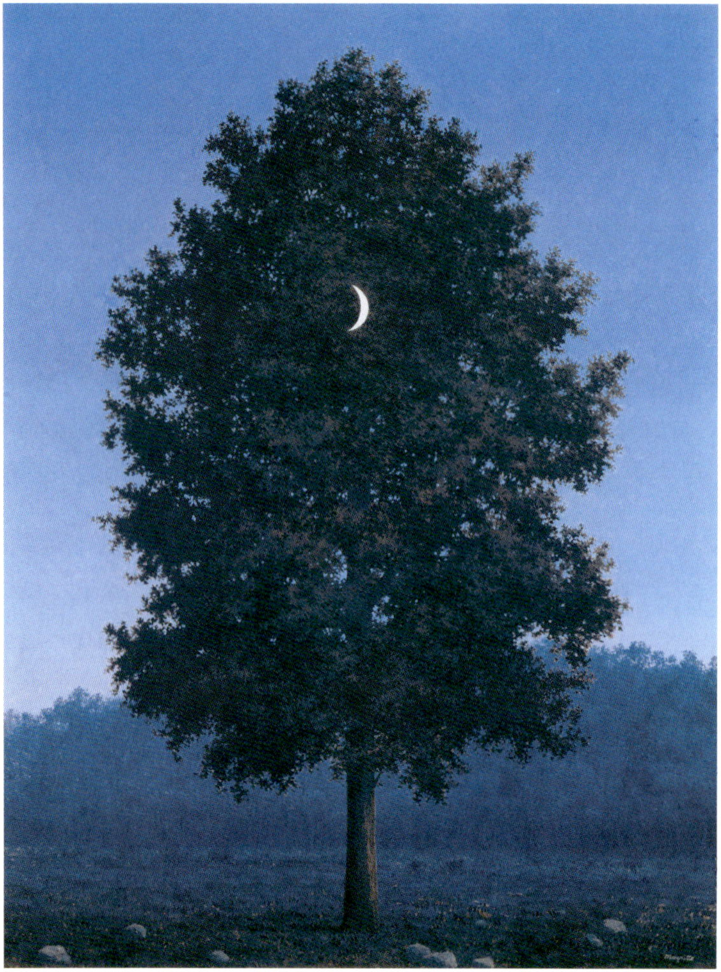

In a letter Magritte wrote to his friends Mirabelle Dors and Maurice Rapin in 1956, he explained, 'I am continuing my "Places au soleil", but the title is no longer appropriate for a large tree in the evening when we see the crescent moon! With this, we have a better, or at least a different, description of *La Place au soleil*: what we see on an object is another object hidden by the one that stands between us and the hidden object.' Here, the moon is visible although hidden by the tree. This procedure was to be reversed in Magritte's last painting, *The Blank Page*, where his declared intention was to superimpose the moon on vegetation.

The Sixteenth of September
1956
Oil on canvas
115 x 88 cm
Koninklijk Museum voor
Schone Kunsten, Antwerp

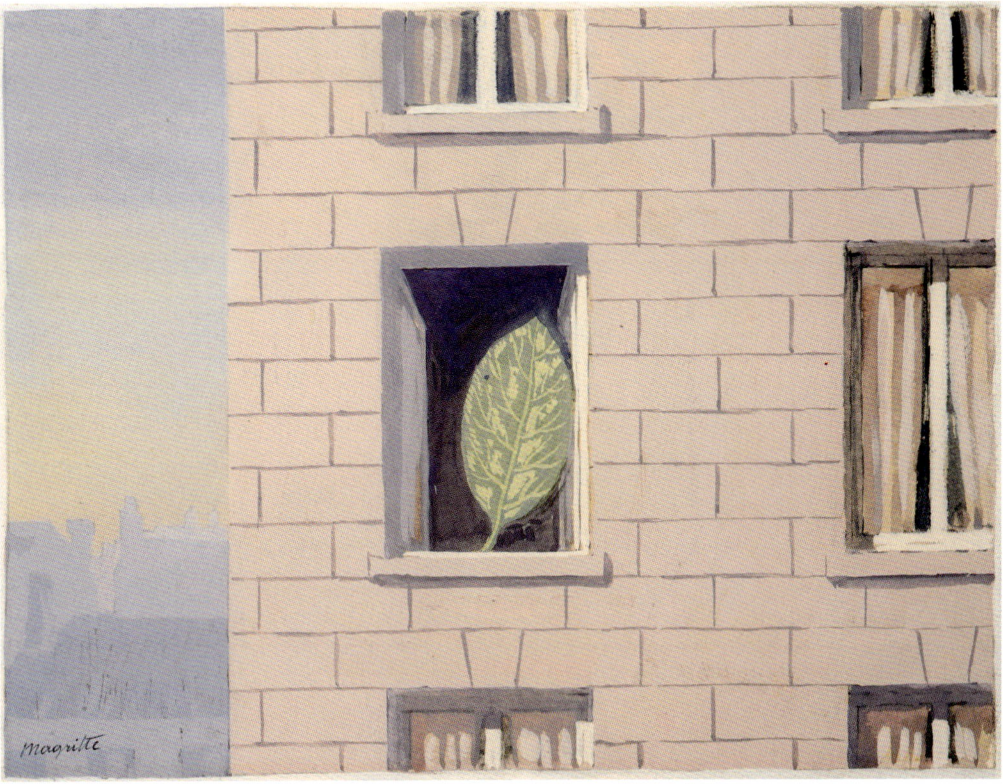

Probably painted in 1958, this gouache recalls *In Praise of the Dialectic* (1937), in which Magritte proposes a solution to the 'problem of the house' by presenting, inside a window, the exterior façade of a dwelling. In this case, the inside/outside dichotomy is preserved by means of a giant leaf 'standing' on the balcony.

The Affable Genius
1958?
Gouache on paper
17.5 x 23.5 cm
Private collection

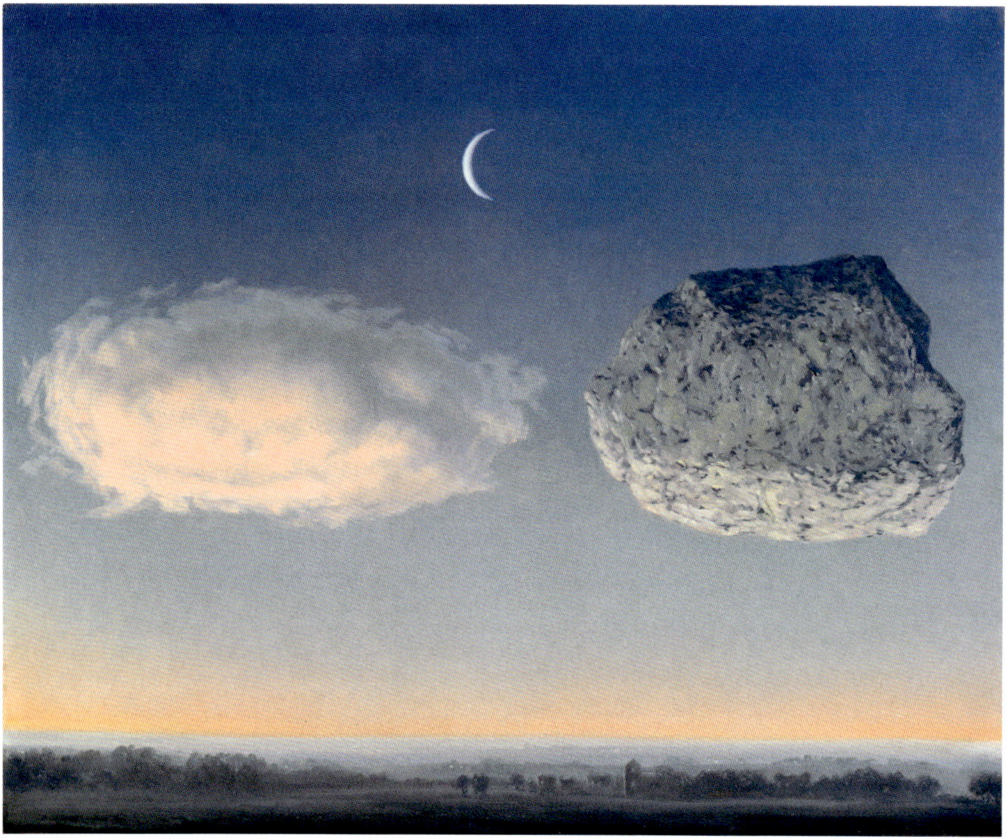

The title, provided by Louis Scutenaire, recalls a hard-fought battle that took place during World War I in the Forest of Argonne, in the north of France. The floating boulder, which reappears the same year in *The Castle in the Pyrenees*, is confronting a cloud here. This miracle, which runs counter to the laws of physics, proclaims the mystery of the world.

The Battle of the Argonne
1959
Oil on canvas
50 x 61 cm
Private collection, Switzerland

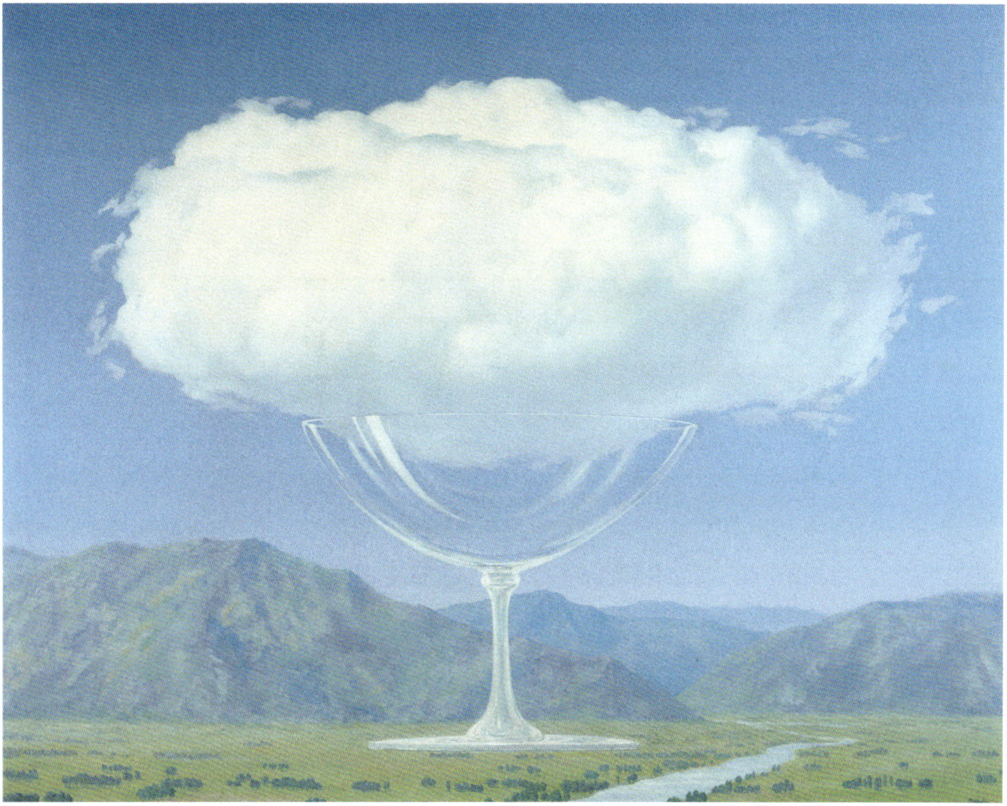

In his problematological approach, Magritte imagined this pictorial solution to the 'problem of the cloud'. The gigantic crystal glass, whose scale is provided by the surrounding landscape, once again attests to the play of proportions Magritte engaged in.

The Heartstring
1960
Oil on canvas
114 x 146 cm
Private collection, Belgium

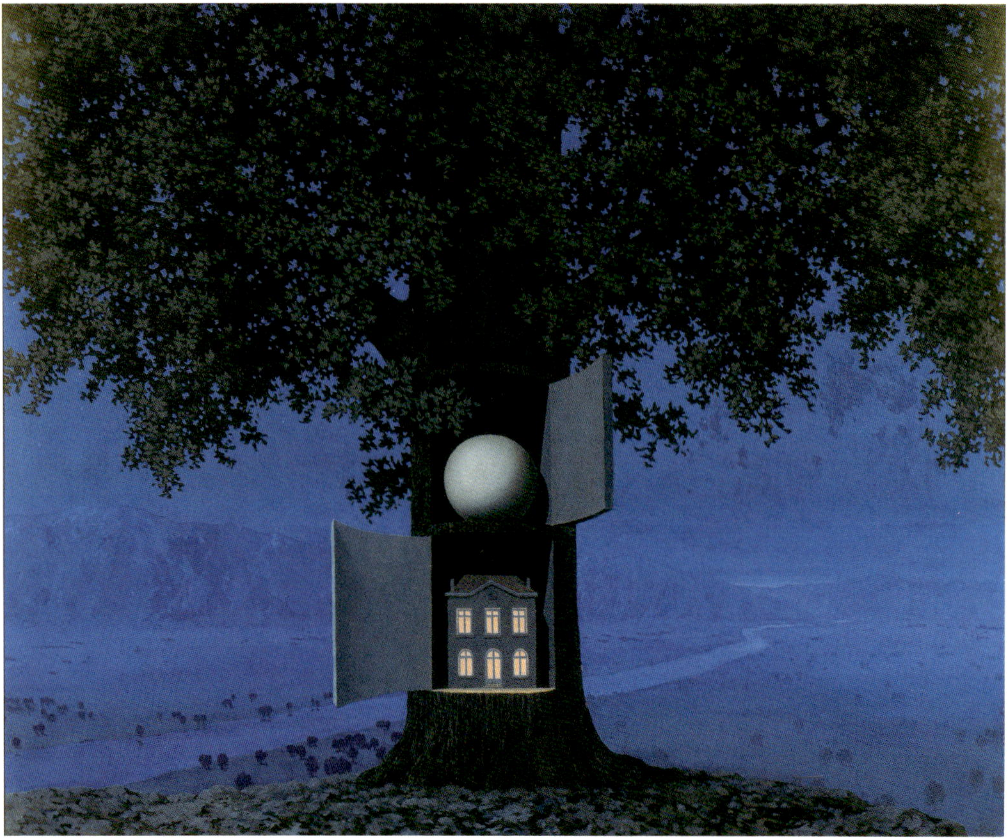

‘The words that blood dictates to us sometimes seem strange. Here apparently it wishes to order us to open magic niches in the trees.’ According to Claude Spaak, Magritte derived this idea from *Alice’s Adventures in Wonderland* (1865) by Lewis Carroll, where there is a tree with ‘a door leading right into it’. This iconography was reused in many variants.

Blood Will Tell
1961
Oil on canvas
90 x 110 cm
Collection Baronne Gillion Crowet

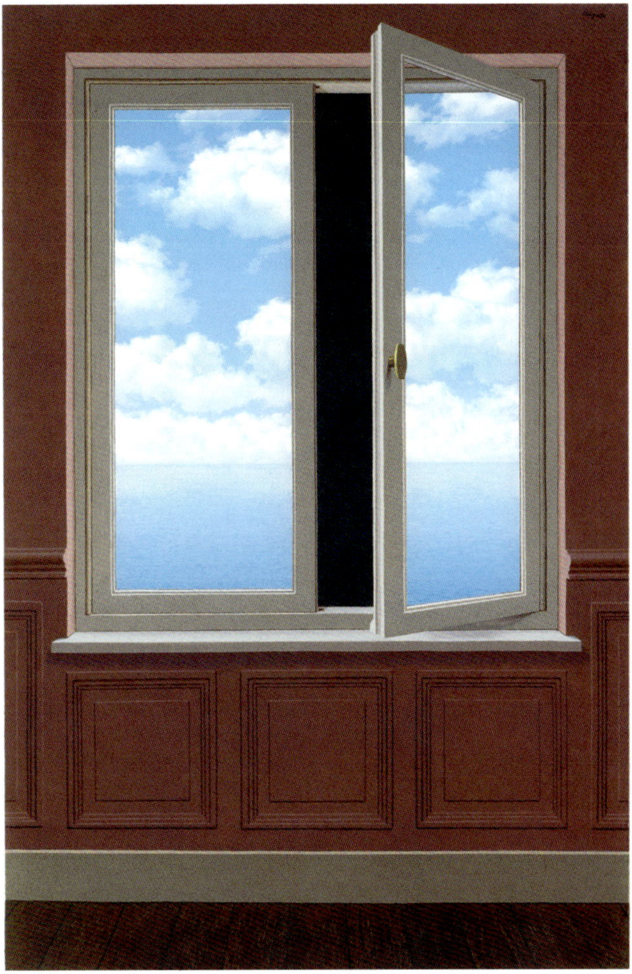

In a letter to André Bosmans in 1962, Magritte described this work as a 'window cracked open on the absence of light' – an absence of light that does not signify the night. 'I myself "experience" this kind of concern when new possibilities with regard to "means" are discovered. Therefore, I am "hesitating" as to the value of the meaning of a colour shown in a painting that is not the colour of an object. I have thought of paintings where one would see black (not the colour of a night sky in this case: through the open window what we see is "blackness" and not the "colour black"). Here, the colour would be that of an object: a black painting.'

The Field-glass
1963
Oil on canvas
175.5 x 116 cm
The Menil Collection, Houston

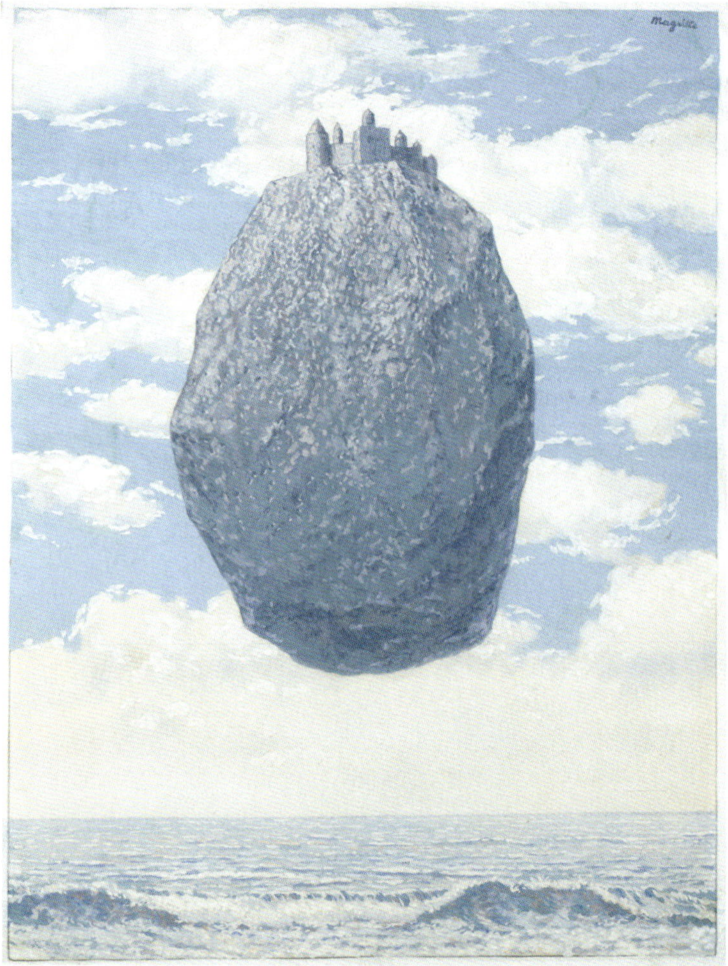

This is a gouache variant of one of Magritte's most emblematic oil paintings. The first version was made in 1959 to hide a window in his friend and confidant Harry Torczyner's New York apartment. Its iconography appears to have been settled upon in a series of letters the two exchanged between February and May 1959.

The Castle in the Pyrenees
1963–1964
Gouache on paper
53.5 x 34.5 cm
Private collection

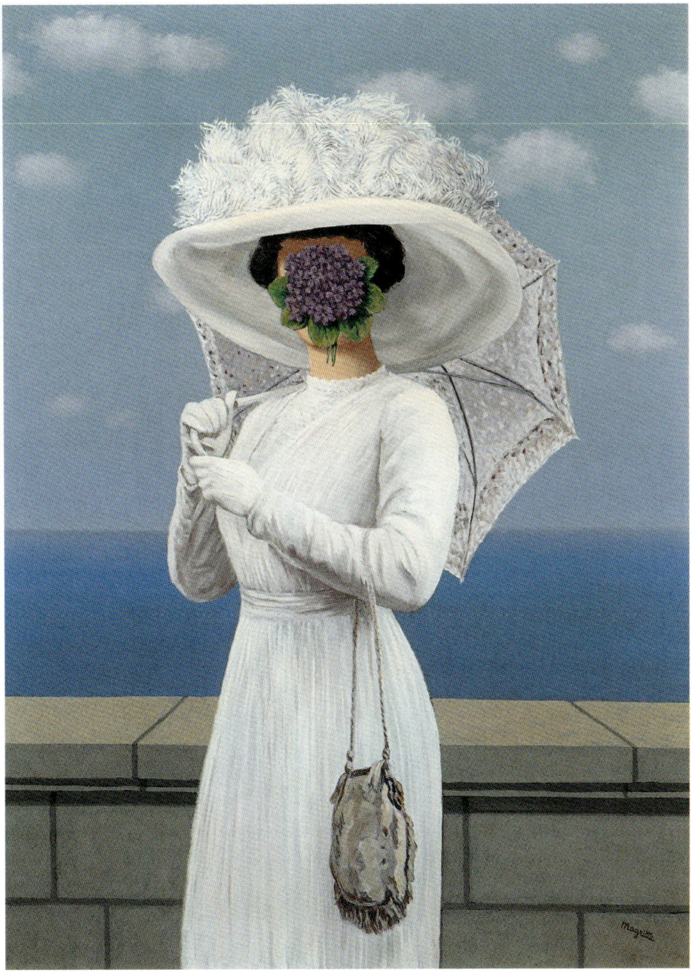

Iconographically, this painting falls within a series initiated by Magritte in 1964 that portrays men and women decked out with an object that obscures their face. The principle of superimposition recalls the series 'La Place au soleil'. The source of inspiration for this canvas may have been a photograph of a performance by the artist Sheila Legge in Trafalgar Square during the International Surrealist Exhibition in 1936. She appeared in a long white dress, her face hidden by a small bouquet of flowers.

The Great War
1964
Oil on canvas
81 x 60 cm
Private collection

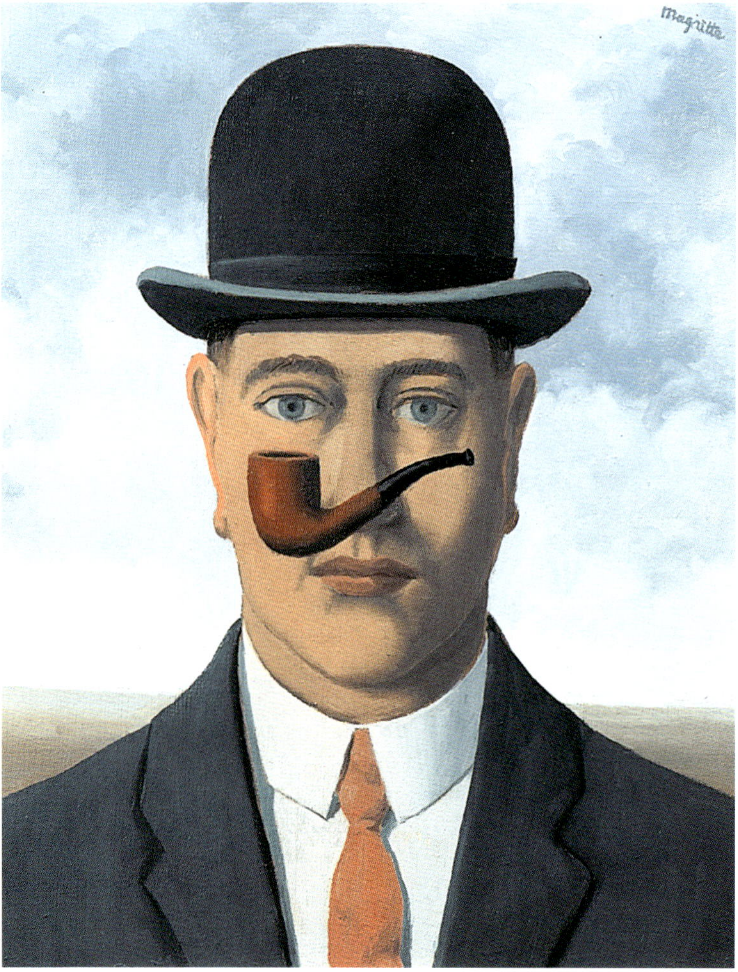

Good Faith is one of a group of works that question the difference between the apparent visible and the hidden visible. As Magritte explained in regard to the famous male counterpart of *The Great War*, 'I take "invisible" to refer to what is not visible – for example heat, weight, pleasure, and so on. There is the *visible that we see*: the apple on the face in "*The Great War*"; and the *hidden visible*: the face hidden by the visible apple.'

Good Faith
1964–1965
Oil on canvas
41 x 33 cm
Private collection

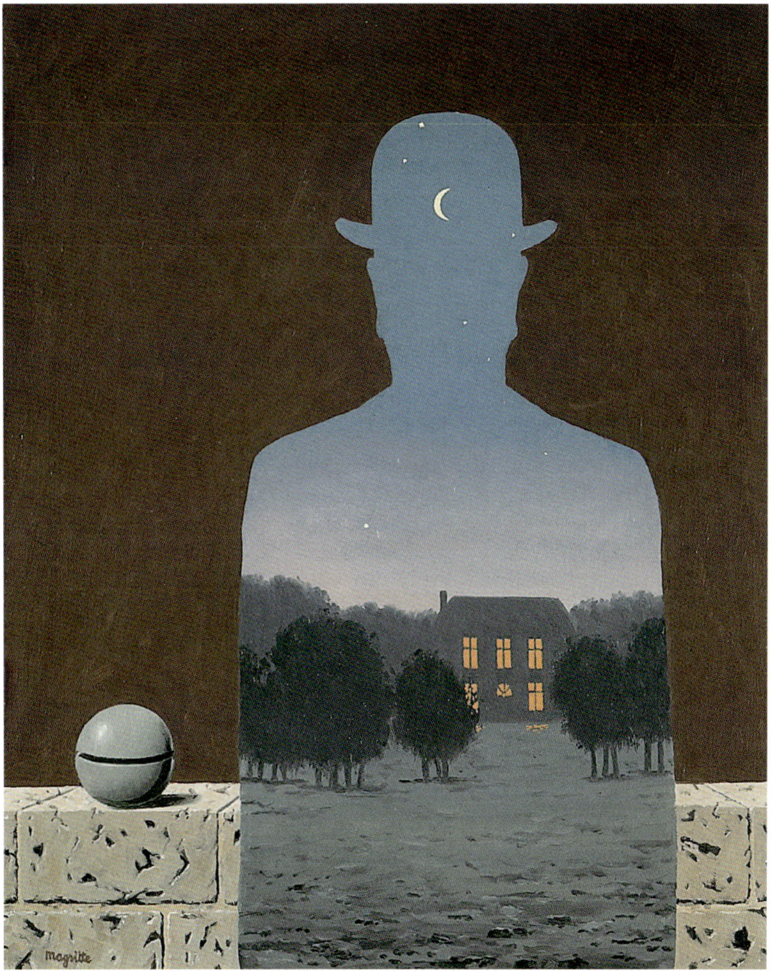

The silhouette of a man wearing a suit and a bowler hat is easily identifiable, although it seems to have absorbed the background landscape, which is reduced to an area of flat brown. This landscape recalls *The Dominion of Light*, but the typically Magritte composition also includes a parapet and a sleigh bell.

The Happy Donor
1966
Oil on canvas
55.5 x 45.5 cm
Museum of Ixelles, Brussels

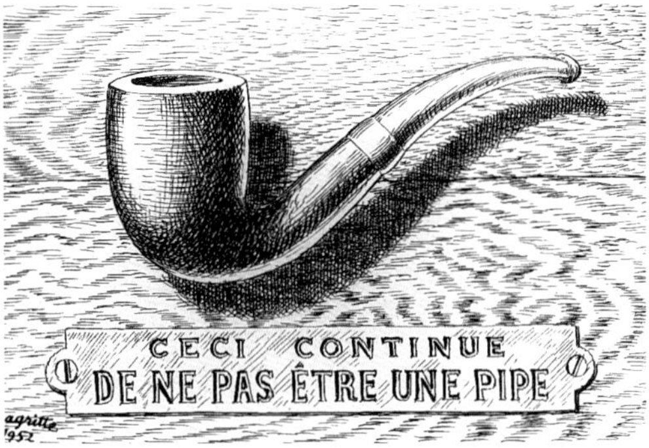

Foreword
Michel Draguet

Text
Julie Waseige

Translation
Donald Pistolesi

Design and typesetting
quod. voor de vorm.

Production
Emiel Godefroit

Printing
DeckersSnoeck

ISBN: 978-94-9181-923-0 – D/2014/6328/12

www.ludion.be